ON DRYDEN'S
ESSAY OF DRAMATIC POESY

FRANK LIVINGSTONE HUNTLEY

UNIVERSITY OF MICHIGAN PRESS

1951

PRINTED IN THE UNITED STATES OF AMERICA
BY J. H. FURST COMPANY, BALTIMORE, MARYLAND

To
KATHARINE

FOREWORD

FOR so important a landmark in English criticism as Dryden's *Essay of Dramatic Poesy*, this study aims to answer such questions as these: What lies behind it? What is its organic unity? Why and how did Dryden defend it? What is its final significance?

Chapter I attempts to synthesize all the available knowledge for our understanding of the text up to the moment of its composition. At the same time it suggests a few new avenues of enquiry.

Chapters II and III present a departure from much that has been written about the *Essay*. Rather than take Dryden's conclusions apart from the rationale of his whole argument, I have assumed that they make their greatest sense within that argument. My Chapter II is not a précis, which in economy and charm would have to give way to Sir Walter Scott's. Other admirably generalized summaries have been written by Ker, Bobertag, Saintsbury, Bohn, Sherwood, and Trowbridge. Instead, this is an analysis of Dryden's argument, and it seeks to determine not only what Dryden is doing in it but why.

In order to obviate many footnotes and to aid the reader who follows the texts, I have incorporated in my paper references to W. P. Ker, *The Essays of John Dryden* (Oxford, 1926), Vol. I. The numbers refer to page and line.

Finally, Chapter IV places the *Essay* and Dryden's thinking about it in a larger setting.

Begun in 1936 at the University of Chicago as part of a doctoral thesis written under the supervision of Professors Ronald S. Crane and George Williamson, this study owes much to them. I am also deeply indebted to my colleague, Professor Louis I. Bredvold, of the University of Michigan.

ANN ARBOR, MICHIGAN
January, 1949

CONTENTS

CHAPTER   PAGE

FOREWORD vii

I. THE BACKGROUND 1

II. THE ARGUMENT 18

III. THE DEFENCE AGAINST HOWARD 57

IV. THE SIGNIFICANCE 68

CHAPTER I

THE BACKGROUND

"My whole discourse was sceptical, according to
that way of reasoning which was used by Socrates,
Plato, and all the Academics of old " (124: 21-24).

THE longest, the most formal, and the most important
piece of Dryden's dramatic criticism is *An Essay of
Dramatic Poesy*. Dryden composed it during an eighteen-
month sojourn at the country estate of the Howards in
Wiltshire during the plague years of 1665-66.[1] It is the only
expression of his criticism unattached to a particular play or
poem, and the only essay which he revised.[2] Three editions
were published during his lifetime—in 1668, 1684, and 1693.
Part of the background for our understanding of the *Essay*
is, then, the relationship it bears to an old quarrel between
the Ancients and the Moderns concerning progress, the
probable sources which Dryden was able to command in his
rural retreat, the identity of the persons in the imagined debate, and its connection with the preface to *Annus Mirabilis*,
which was composed at approximately the same time and in
the same place.

[1] Probably from June, 1665. through December. 1666; cf. Hugh Macdonald.
John Dryden: A Bibliography of Early Editions and of Drydeniana (Oxford.
1939), p. 13. The *Essay* was registered at Stationers' Hall on August 7. 1667
(Eyre and Rivington, II, 380, *Transcript of Registers . . . 1640-1708* A.D.
[London, 1913-14], II, 380).
[2] The revisions first appeared in the 1684 edition (Macdonald. *op. cit.*,
No. 127 b ii, p. 165). The *Essay* has received distinguished editing. notably
by Robert Urie in 1750; Edmund Malone. 1800; Sir Walter Scott. 1808; Edward
Arber, 1880; George Saintsbury. 1882; Thomas Arnold. 1889; William Strunk.
1898; and W. P. Ker, 1900.

1

In the century before Dryden was born, both Italy and France had come to believe in the worth of their native literatures. Tassoni's *Pensieri* (1612-20) argued the superiority of Italian letters to Homer and Virgil, a concept quickly translated into French by Baudouin. From this, Boisrobert, Desmarest, and others exalted French writers above the Ancients, and Perrault wrote *Le Siècle de Louis le Grand* as proof of French national greatness in literature and also in general knowledge. As the quarrel over Corneille's *Le Cid* echoed through the century, it became a question not so much of literary history, of rules and verse, as of whether or not there is progress in the forward march of mankind in time.[3] For the understanding of the relation of these ideas to Dryden's *Essay*, Professor Williamson's article on its genesis is indispensable.[4]

Dryden, as an English man of letters in 1665, knew that a generation before him in France *Le Cid* had withstood the attempts of the Ancients to weigh it on Aristotle's supposed scales and find it wanting. Some of his compatriots preferred the ancient Greek to English plays, and others taxed English plays with being looser in construction than the French. To admit their views would be to argue for retrogression, from greatness in the culture of Greece and Rome to paltriness in that of England—England, which had just restored to the throne an urbane and witty monarch, England, which had just defeated the great Dutch fleet. And yet we have profited by the work of the Ancients. Thus Dryden adopts the sceptical attitude as he too carries on the famous controversy on progress. Defending his patriotic epilogue only four years later, he wrote: " For we live in an age so sceptical, that as it determines little, so it takes nothing from antiquity on trust; and I profess to have no other ambition in this

---

[3] Cf. the studies of Rigault, Gillot, Gasté, and Guthkelch for the French controversy; and R. F. Jones for its passage to England.

[4] George Williamson, "The Occasion of *An Essay of Dramatic Poesy*," *Modern Philology*, 44 (1946), 1-9. Williamson has discovered the occasion in the quarrel between Sprat and Sorbière on the comparative merits of English and French literature. The " ingenious person of our nation " (61: 8-9) Williamson identifies with Thomas Sprat.

Essay, than that poetry may not go backward, when all other arts and sciences are advancing" (163: 1-6).

Related as the *Essay* is to a contemporary controversy among French and English men of letters, it would be strange indeed were Dryden to have written his contribution without any sources whatsoever. And yet accusations of plagiarism are so rife in Drydeniana that they must be looked upon with the same kind of scepticism that Professor Bredvold, in *The Intellectual Milieu of John Dryden* (1934), has traced for Dryden. Langbaine, inveterate source hunter, had to confess that, though he was sure Dryden had stolen, the man could still conceal what he had borrowed far better than Jonson could.[5] In the *Defence of an "Essay of Dramatic Poesy,"* Dryden himself referred to his *Essay* as "a little discourse in dialogue, for the most part borrowed from the observations of others" (112: 19-21), which is obvious understatement. Another confession of indebtedness in the same defence serves merely to put Dryden on the side of the best authorities: "Those propositions which are laid down in my discourse as helps to the better imitation of Nature, are not mine (as I have said), nor were ever pretended so to be, but derived from the authority of Aristotle and Horace, and from the rules and examples of Ben Jonson and Corneille (125: 25-30)." It is even part of the sceptical tradition to admit borrowing in order to lend universality. "*Plutarke* would peradventure tell us," Montaigne wrote, "of that which he hath written, that it is the worke of others, that his examples are in all and everie where true. . . ."[6]

Contemporaries insisted, however, that Dryden had borrowed much from the Spanish critics and from the French. Joseph Spence, for example, reported that Bolingbroke had told him that Dryden had "got more from the Spanish critics alone, than from the Italian and French, and all other critics put together."[7] Spence's quotation of Bolingbroke

[5] Gerard Langbaine, *An Account of the English Dramatick Poets* (Oxford, 1691), p. 148.

[6] M. E. de Montaigne. "Of the Force of Imagination," Book I, Chap. XX; Everyman's Library, I, 104.

[7] *Anecdotes, Observations and Characters of Books and Men . . .* ([1728-30] 2d ed., London, 1858), p. 11, in a note signed "B" [Bolingbroke].

was published some fifty years after the *Essay* was written, and Bolingbroke was only twenty-two years old when Dryden died. Spence's reference, also, makes no specific mention of *An Essay of Dramatic Poesy.* Nevertheless, W. P. Ker [8] held to the opinion that Tirso de Molina's *Cigarrales de Toledo* might be a source of Dryden's dialogue. Langbaine, who would not give Dryden more credit than he deserved, admitted often that Dryden had read too much Spanish literature.[9] Shadwell, in the "Epistle to the Tories," wrote: "Whoever has been conversant with Spanish, Italian, French and Classick Authors, will find all that's tollerably good in him in some of those; he can, indeed, new trim, and disguise a little, the Clothes he steals." [10]   Another contemporary, Martin Clifford, tells us that Dryden was well acquainted with *Don Quixote.*[11]

Some modern scholars, however, conclude, perhaps hastily, that Dryden could not even read Spanish. Allison Gaw believes that Dryden's *Wild Gallant* was adapted from Spanish only through the medium of Sir Samuel Tuke: "This unmistakable evidence that the *Wild Gallant* was not a translation from the Spanish removes the only piece of evidence of any weight supporting the belief that John Dryden had a reading knowledge of Spanish." [12]   And after an examination of the Spanish sources of Dryden's comedies, Ned Allen states: "If he really knew the Spanish critics as well as Spence's anecdote would indicate, it seems odd that this knowledge is not revealed in *An Essay of Dramatic Poesy* or in his other essays." [13]   Similarly, with a possible misunderstanding

---

[8] W. P. Ker, *The Essays of John Dryden* (Oxford, 1926), Introd., p. xxxvi.

[9] Cf. his discussion of "The Conquest of Granada," in *An Account of the English Dramatick Poets* (Oxford, 1691), pp. 158-159.

[10] *The Medal of John Bayes* (London, 1682), A 1 verso.

[11] *Notes upon Mr. Dryden's Poems in Four Letters* ([1674] London, 1687), p. 19.

[12] "Tuke's *Adventures of Five Hours* in Relation to the 'Spanish Plot' and to John Dryden," *Publications of the University of Pennsylvania,* Studies in English Drama, Series in Philology and Literature, 14 (1917), 16, n. 35. I have long been convinced that Dryden could read Spanish well. Further positive evidence has recently been brought to light by J. U. Rundle, "The Source of Dryden's 'Comic Plot' in *The Assignation*," *Modern Philology,* 45 (1947), 104-111.

[13] *The Sources of John Dryden's Comedies* (Ann Arbor, 1935), p. 6, n. 22.

of Dryden's ground, Louis E. Friedland writes: "Strong Spanish influence has been claimed for him by Bolingbroke, though if [this] were true, Dryden would inevitably have reflected, more certainly than he does, the Spanish desire for liberty in the drama." [14] In his study of Spanish and English literatures, Martin Hume finds no influence of Spanish criticism in England. [15] As a climax of this negative review of scholarship on the problem of Dryden's Spanish sources here, Morel-Fatio finds in the *Essay* very little of the Spanish theater — "quelques allusions, rien de plus." [16] And he prints a personal letter in which Ker gives up Tirso de Molina but "still hanker[s] after the *Arte* [of Lope de Vega] as a possible source of some of Dryden's views." Morel-Fatio adds, without break:

. . . Que Dryden ait connu les passages du Don Quichotte relatifs au théâtre, c'est très probable; qu'il ait connu l'*Arte* de Lope, c'est possible; néanmoins, je ne pense pas que le propos que lui attribue lord Bolingbroke soit autre chose qu'une boutade. A une allusion faite dans une conversation à ses emprunts aux critiques italiens et français, il aura dû répondre un peu vivement, pour les atténuer: 'Mais je dois beaucoup plus aux Espagnols . . . ,' et ses interlocuteurs n'y ont pas été voir. [17]

Spence's anecdote, if true, appears to describe a quip given by a tired old man to a fresh young literary aspirant. And yet a cursory reading of Spanish criticism with the aid of Schack and Menéndez y Pelayo reveals many an interesting sidelight on the possibility of truth in Bolingbroke's remark. I have found no Spanish source, that is, no piece of formal criticism the major problem of which is identical with that of the *Essay* and solved in the same way. But the controversy in Spain over Lope de Vega's comedies must have been known to Dryden, and the spirit of Lope's *Arte* is that of Dryden's *Essay*—a desire for freedom from foreign shackles, and a passion to please the public. It is just as probable that

[14] Louis E. Friedland, "Dramatic Unities in England," *Journal of English and Germanic Philology*, 10 (1911), 298.

[15] Martin A. S. Hume, *Spanish Influence on English Literature* (London. 1895; Philadelphia, 1905). Nothing was found in the works of similar nature by F. H. Ristine and by George Ticknor.

[16] "Les Défenseurs de la Comedia," *Bulletin Hispanique*, 4 (1902), 33.

[17] *Ibid.*, p. 36, note.

the lack of regularity in Lope's system is responsible for Dryden's not using it more as a source. Tirso de Molina's defence of Lope in *Los Cigarrales de Toledo*[18] was published twelve years before Corneille's *Cid*. Ciramuel's commentary on the *Arte* appeared only two years before Dryden wrote the *Essay*. Against Lope were a host of "regulars." Cascales, for one, in his *Tablas* asks a question on the mixing of mirth and tragedy that might have been asked by Crites: "¿Como queréis concertar a Heraclito y a Democrito? El trágico mueve a terror y misericordia: el cómico mueve a risa."[19] Certainly a parallel to the division of the parts of a play by Crites into plot and language is this definition by Pinciano: "El poema es un compuesto de alma (fábula) y cuerpo (lenguaje)."[20] All the familiar critical concepts emerge from this body of Spanish criticism, especially the almost inescapable dichotomy of "nature" and "art." But who can tell that Dryden ever saw any of them? The running down of parallels and sources carries one far afield; yet it is not safe to say that Dryden got nothing from the Spanish critics. One can only conclude that his Spanish sources are not as obvious as his quotations from Corneille.

As for French sources, Edmund Malone[21] mentions Martin Clifford's accusation that Dryden's essay was stolen from Hedelin, Mesnardiere, and Corneille.[22] My own comparison of d'Aubignac's *La Pratique du Théâtre* (1657) and Mesnardière's *Poétique* (1640) with the *Essay* reveals practically nothing that can be called source material.[23]

But there can be no doubt that, as Dryden readily admits

[18] M. Menéndez y Pelayo, *Historia de las idéas estéticas en España* (Madrid, 1884-91), III, 465.

[19] *Ibid.*, p. 361.

[20] *Ibid.*, p. 332.

[21] Edmund Malone, *The Critical and Miscellaneous Prose Works of John Dryden* (London, 1800), I, Part II, 33.

[22] *Notes upon Mr. Dryden's Poems in Four Letters*, at the end of the second letter, p. 8: "I was about six years since a little acquainted with a Name-sake and Countrey-man of yours who pilfer'd out of Monsieur *Hedelin, Menardiere,* and *Corneill* an Essay of Dramatick Poetry, wherein he tells us another tale and says, *a Play ought to be a just and Lively Image of Humane Nature, Representing its Passions and Humours,* &c. . . . Si sic omnia dixisset."

[23] Ker arrived at similarly negative conclusions (*op. cit.*, Introd., pp. xxxvi-xxxvii). Cf. also Friedland, *op. cit.*, p. 298.

in the *Essay* itself, he leaned heavily for ideas and examples upon the *Trois Discours* which Corneille had affixed to the 1660 edition of his plays.[24] Several scholars have studied the parallels and quotations. Ker concluded: " Dryden was going through a similar progress in his own views about his work, and Corneille's discussion of principles must have seemed to him in many places the echo of his own thoughts."[25] Apropos of the *Essay*, Friedland noted that Corneille saw the *liaison des scènes* not as a rule but as an ornament, and that this is the source of the concept in Dryden.[26] For the dramatic unities in particular, Dryden owed most, according to Friedland, to Ben Jonson; nevertheless, from Corneille " he received the original impulse to critical thought and 'a quickening of interest in critical discussion.' "[27] A. F. B. Clarke concluded that only in the *Essay* is there explicit borrowing, but that the other prefaces show an indebtedness in spirit to Corneille: " Though there is no explicit borrowing from Corneille in Dryden's other essays on dramatic subjects,[28] they are nearly all characterized by that judicial balancing between the rules and the artistic need of individual liberty which the author no doubt learned from Corneille's *Discours*."[29] Dorothy Burrows, in her unpublished dissertation entitled " The Relation of Dryden's Serious Plays and Dramatic Criticism to Contemporary French Literature " (University of Illinois, 1933), has painstakingly gathered allusions in the *Essay* to Corneille and set them down with the parallel French text Apparently without availing himself of Miss Burrows' spadework, Pierre Legouis,[30] too, has made a discriminating study of the parallels between the *Essay* and Corneille's *Discours*.

Granted that Dryden included some passages from Cor-

---

[24] The text I have used is that of Pierre Corneille, *Œuvres*, ed. Charles Marty-Laveaux, 12 vols. (Paris, 1862), Vol. I.

[25] *Op. cit.*, Introd., pp. xxxviii-xxxix.

[26] Friedland, *op. cit.*, p. 282.

[27] *Ibid.*, p. 298.

[28] He excepts the passage in Ker, *op. cit.*, II, 157-158.

[29] *Boileau and the French Classical Critics in England, 1660-1830* (Paris, 1925), p. 242. Cf. also A. M. Ellis, " Horace's Influence on Dryden," *Philological Quarterly*, 4 (1925), 46-52.

[30] Pierre Legouis, " Corneille and Dryden as Dramatic Critics," *Seventeenth Century Studies Presented to Sir Herbert Grierson* (Oxford, 1938), pp. 269-291.

neille and other French critics in the *Essay*, the larger questions of why he quotes them at particular junctures in his argument and what use he makes of them remain. Dryden's dependence upon and divergence from Corneille is part of his argument, to be considered in the next chapter.

Sceptical and general though Dryden's discourse is, whatever the sources, the next question in the background which requires some answer is whether or not the characters in the dialogue are identifiable with actual persons whom he knew.[31] Dryden himself tells us near the beginning of his *Essay* that "three of them [are] persons whom their wit and quality have made known to all the town; and whom I have chose to hide under these borrowed names" (28:21–29:2). With this as his starting point, Malone wrote a long account identifying the persons with actual people.[32] Almost everyone[33] who has worked with the *Essay* since 1800 has taken for granted Malone's identification of the four speakers: Crites as Sir Robert Howard; Eugenius as Charles Sackville, Lord Buckhurst, later Earl of Dorset; Lisideius as Sir Charles Sedley; and Neander as Dryden himself.

No more than it will be known exactly what historical persons lie behind the names in the dialogues of Plato and of T. S. Eliot can we ever discover to what extent Dryden had actual friends in his mind when he conceived his characters in this dialogue. Yet, from the *entretiens* of Sarrasin and of Desmarest Dryden knew well the heuristic value of bringing together various speakers, each presenting a different point of view, to discuss the principles of dramatic poesy.

Perhaps a mistake has been made in concentrating more on Dryden's "three persons of quality" than on his insistence that he had chosen to "hide [them] under these bor-

---

[31] See my article " On the Persons in Dryden's *Essay of Dramatic Poesy*," *Modern Language Notes*, 63 (1948), 88-95, where the suggestions are treated with greater fullness and documentation.

[32] Malone, *op. cit.*, Vol. I, Part II. Cf. the summary in Macdonald, *Bibliography* (see note 1), p. 165, n. i.

[33] Cf., for example, Churton Collins, *Essays and Studies* (London, 1895), p. 30; Ker, *op. cit.*, Introd., p. xxxvii; J. N. Smith and E. W. Parks, *The Great Critics* (New York, 1939), p. 304; James M. Osborn, *John Dryden: Some Biographical Facts and Problems* (New York, 1940), pp. 29, 57, *et passim*.

rowed names." Too great an anxiety to accept as fact the hypothesis that his persons are portraits may have prevented us from perceiving the general, allegorical functions of the speakers in the dialogue.

Crites, the first speaker, shows most obviously the half-portrait of Howard and the half-dramatic function. On the grounds of the coincidence of some of Crites' opinions and those of Sir Robert Howard's published work, Malone settled on this identification. For over a hundred years it was never called in question. In 1923 G. R. Noyes pointed out that in Howard's prefaces Sir Robert (1) attacks the use of rime in drama, (2) argues for the preëminence of English drama over that of Greece and Rome, and (3) attacks the authority of the three unities.[34] Of these views, however, the Crites of the *Essay* advances only the first and differs radically from the second and the third. It is not surprising that the literary quarrel between Dryden and his brother-in-law centered on the use of rime in drama since, in literature and not in temperament, this was the one issue between them.

The name Crites is appropriate for a person whose dramatic function in the dialogue is that of a carping criticaster. Since the purpose of the whole essay was " chiefly to vindicate the honour of our English writers " (27: 12-15), the character to oppose the English and the modern point of view had to be a Crites. Simple though this may be, no other explanation can adequately show us why, if Dryden intended Crites to be his brother-in-law Sir Robert Howard, he made him so different in many of his views from Sir Robert. Crites, therefore, is as much a character in a play as he is a portrait.

If Noyes's animadversions on Crites are admitted, then Malone's identifications of the other characters can also be challenged, as his grounds for them are far less tenable. Eugenius is the second speaker. Malone[35] identifies him with Charles Lord Buckhurst (later the sixth Earl of Dorset) on the sole ground that Matthew Prior, in the dedication of

---

[34] "'Crites' in Dryden's *Essay of Dramatic Poesy*," *Modern Language Notes*, 38 (1923), 333-337.
[35] I, ii, 62.

his 1709 edition of *Poems* to Lionel, Earl of Dorset, acclaimed Lionel's father as the Eugenius of Dryden's *Essay*. This single proof is taken from a preface conceived in a spirit of glowing encomium forty years after the *Essay* was published.

That Eugenius is not Buckhurst, however, is more probable. Dryden had dedicated his *Essay* to Lord Buckhurst as a neutral arbiter in the argument. Yet Eugenius, far from being impartial, is definitely on Neander's side (35: 20-30). The long passage (Ker, II, 16-17) in Dryden's dedication to the same Lord Buckhurst of his essay on *Satire* in 1693, which links his noble patron once more to the *Essay of Dramatic Poesy*, makes no mention of Buckhurst as the Eugenius of the *Essay*, in spite of ample rhetorical occasion. Neither of the two surviving letters written by Dryden to Buckhurst mentions the identification with Eugenius.[36] Finally, Charles Sackville Lord Buckhurst had volunteered in the fleet fitted out against the Dutch, and had taken part in the naval battle of June 3, 1665.[37] Would Dryden's sense of drama, while allowing him to dedicate the *Essay* to an absent friend and patron, have allowed him to include that absent friend in an imagined colloquy whose setting and dramatic occasion is the very day of that battle? Rather, Eugenius, the "well-born one," stands as a symbol throughout the *Essay* of the man of quality who has good taste. Little more can be gained by thinking of him as Lord Buckhurst.

Malone's grounds for identifying the third speaker, Lisideius, with Sir Charles Sedley are (1) that Sedley was a friend of Buckhurst; (2) that Sedley was a great voluptuary, and at the end of the dialogue, while the graver Neander and Crites go home to bed, the two others seek the pleasure of the town; and (3) that Lisideius is an anagram for Sidleyius, the Latinized form of the variant spelling of the name Sedley.

But what is Lisideius' function? He gives the definition of a play, which is the starting point of the whole argument

[36] Cf. Charles E. Ward, *The Letters of John Dryden* (Durham, N. C., 1942), No. 6 (*c.* 1677) and No. 22 (*c.* 1691).
    [37] *Dictionary of National Biography*, L, 87. Cf. Brice Harris, *Charles Sackville, Sixth Earl of Dorset* (Illinois Studies in Language and Literature, 26, Nos. 3-4, Urbana, Illinois, 1940), pp. 33-34.

and its primary source of unity. Also, he is the first to uphold the Moderns (the French rather than the English) in a debate between the Ancients and the Moderns. He begins his speech with Corneille (56: 26-32), and throughout his argument there is constant and frank allusion to Corneille's *Trois Discours*. His very name does not appear on the surface to be as clearly Greek as the names Crites, Eugenius, and Neander.

For these reasons we may well look towards France and especially to Corneille for a clue to the origin of Lisideius. Is it rash to suggest, therefore, that in honor of the protagonist in the notorious controversy in France over *Le Cid*, the name Lisideius may have come to Dryden from an Anglicized pronunciation of "Le Cid" plus a Latinized Greek masculine ending?

And how do we know that Neander was intended to be Dryden himself? Neander's views certainly come closest to Dryden's own. Malone was also led to the identification by the anagram on Dryden's name.[38] "Neander" was used for Dryden in the *Luctus Britannici* (1700) and in Mrs. Thomas' *Poems* of 1727 [39] — both instances of complimentary metaphor.

Although Neander uses many of Dryden's own arguments, he is almost as inconsistently Dryden's mouthpiece as Crites is Sir Robert's. In the first edition of the *Essay* Dryden uses direct address (89: 32) in passing from his second to his third main section; and here he uses "I," meaning himself apart from Neander, and "my Lord," meaning Buckhurst apart from Eugenius. In the *Defence*, too, Dryden distinguished between his own views and those of his imaginary character: " . . . several persons maintained their several opinions . . . ; he who answered, in behalf of our nation, was willing to give more latitude to the rule . . . . In few words my own opinion is this " (130: 19-26). In spite of Dryden's insistence upon the sceptical spirit of his *essai*, his literal-

---

[38] I, ii, 34 n., 63, 118. Malone has a fairly strong argument in his quotation from the *Essay* (94: 6-7) on Neander's writing of verse.

[39] Cf. Macdonald, *op. cit.*, p. 165, n. 1. The Mrs. Thomas is, of course, the "Corinna" who gave the world the extravagant account of Dryden's funeral.

minded brother-in-law took everything Crites said as directed towards himself and everything Neander said as coming straight from Dryden. That Neander's views are closest to Dryden's own, however, is merely to say that Dryden himself represents the new against the old. In a discourse that concerns the idea of progress in letters "Neander" may be allegorically simply the "new man," from *neo* and *aner*, *andros*, as his name implies. So much for the persons in the dialogue. Though they may very well be partially portraits, concentration on Malone's identifications obscures their dramatic functions in Dryden's imagined debate.

The account of *Annus Mirabilis* which Dryden wrote to his brother-in-law, dated from Charlton, Wiltshire, November 10, 1666, was written at approximately the same time and at the same place to the very person who is partially the Crites of the *Essay*. This preface, therefore, will have to be analyzed, finally, as part of the background material. Registered on January 21, 1667, it serves to solve a problem common to drama and poetry: How are the words of a " poem" to be made appropriate to the thoughts? In it Dryden first developed several distinctions — for example, that between the contriving of a poem and its writing — which in the *Essay* he applies to a play. It also introduces us to Dryden's mode of thinking, so characteristic of the neoclassical age, in pairs of universal terms whose meanings complement each other (like " nature" and " art") and constantly shift in significance. The earlier preface, moreover, illustrates in smaller compass Dryden's habitual treatment of literature, largely derived from Horace and Quintilian, as rhetoric—in terms of the poet, the medium, and the audience. In this mode the problems of criticism, as of rhetoric, are usually those of the aims the artist should achieve and his inherent and acquired capacities to succeed in them, the ends and rules (for plot, style, etc.) of the work, and the qualities of taste and training of the particular audience whom the artist is addressing.

Dryden begins his account of " *The Year of Wonders* " with its subject matter, obviously because a poet chooses the subject first, then puts it into verse. It is the subject of the naval battle with the Dutch of June 1-4, 1666 (that with which his *Essay* opens occurred the preceding year), and the great fire of London, one event chronologically subsequent to the other.[40]   This subject, in Dryden's dialectic, he later equates with the "thoughts" of a poem, as distinct from the "words."   Without a break in his paragraph, he goes on to speak of two other matters inseparable from his subject: the category of his poem and the choice of stanza. Because the action of the poem is not single, arranged in an order of cause and effect that might bring about a conclusion as in a plot, he places his poem in the historical category of the *Pharsalia* rather than in the epic category of the *Punica* (11: 19-20). The choice of stanza depends upon its suitability to the subject matter and occasion (12: 9-16) — a position which he maintains in the *Essay* for using heroic couplet in heroic drama and for abandoning the heroic couplet ten years later when he attempted to imitate the style of Shakespeare in *All for Love*. As in a speech, again, the purpose and the occasion largely control the style.

The problem of making words appropriate to thoughts is more than one of choosing a stanzaic form or of describing sea fights in exact nautical terms. Dryden's enthusiasm for his subject leads him into a digression. But it is important to let the reader know that the finding of the subject and the inspiration of thoughts that subject gives largely took care of themselves; the poet's real work was the adorning of those thoughts with elocution (14: 17-20).

Thus the key passage in the preface distinguishes between "wit writing," the faculty in the poet which suits the thoughts to the subject, and "wit written," the finished product as it exists in the poem. Called by Ker "one of the most systematic passages in Dryden,"[41] it deserves quotation in full:

The composition of all poems is, or ought to be, of wit; and wit in the poet, or *Wit writing*, (if you will give me leave to use a school-distinction), is no other than the faculty of imagination in the writer, which, like a

---

[40] For the political implications see E. N. Hooker. " The Purpose of Dryden's *Annus Mirabilis*," *Huntington Library Quarterly*, 10 (1946), 49-67.
[41] Ker, *op. cit.*, I, 287.

nimble spaniel,[42] beats over and ranges through the field of memory, till it springs the quarry it hunted after; or, without metaphor, which searches over all the memory for the species or ideas of those things which it designs to represent. *Wit written* is that which is well defined, the happy result of thought, or product of imagination [14: 21-30].[43]

The beginning of the paragraph (14: 17) marks the two main divisions of Dryden's essay: certain essentials in the poem which must exactly fit the thoughts, and elocution or the happy result. This, then, is the first answer to his main problem: the " proper wit " of a heroic or historical poem is " delightful imagining of persons, actions, passions, or things " (14: 32-34). The " wit written," or result of the poetic faculty, is not a kind of specious adornment, specious in that it is neither " apt " nor " lively "—like epigrams, puns, antitheses. Rather, " it is some lively and apt description, dressed in such colours of speech, that it sets before your eyes the absent object, as perfectly, and more delightfully than nature " (15: 5-8). This definition gives us the first statement of two important canons in Dryden's future dramatic criticism. The correlative and complementary terms " lively " and " apt " foreshadow the definition of a play in *An Essay of Dramatic Poesy* as a " just and lively image of human nature " (36: 5). And it anticipates Dryden's setting of " delight " through liveliness over and above the criterion of verisimilitude. Such a hierarchy of ends is ordained by the nature of the art which Dryden describes. To be more than merely " just " or " apt " in one's representation of nature is impossible; but it is possible and therefore the poet's duty to make his imitation more delightful than the object by means of " wit written."

Under the " lively and apt description " Dryden arranges three " happinesses " of the poet's imagination, which echo

[42] Dryden repeats this simile of the spaniel from 8: 7-9. Cf. Hobbes, *Leviathan*, Book I, Chap. 3 (Everyman's Library, p. 10), in the chapter " Of the Consequences of Trayne of Imagination ": " or as a Spaniel ranges the field, till he find a sent."

[43] T. S. Eliot, " A Note on Two Odes of Cowley," *Seventeenth Century Studies Presented to Sir Herbert Grierson* (Oxford, 1938), pp. 238 ff., makes a comparison of this passage with Cowley's ode and with Dr. Johnson's dicta on wit.

the three major terms of classical rhetoric: *inventio, dispositio,* and *elocutio.* The first is invention, or the finding of the thought (15: 8-10). Its property is "quickness of the imagination." The second is fancy or "the variation, deriving, or moulding of that thought, as the judgment represents it proper to the subject" (15: 10-12). It makes for fertility. So far these happinesses of the poet's genius expand what Dryden had written in his very first essay of the fancy moving images from darkness to light and of the judgment selecting certain images and rejecting others (1: 1-8) — doctrine more Platonic than Aristotelian. The third happiness of the poet's imagination is elocution, or "the art of clothing and adorning that thought, so found and varied, in apt, significant, and sounding words" (15: 12-15). Its property is "accuracy in expression." These three rhetorical terms are woven throughout the other set of basic terms: poetry, the poet, the particular poem, and the appreciative audience.[44] When the poet is discussed, for example, his genius is assigned to *inventio,* his judgment to a combination of *dispositio* and *elocutio.* When the poem is being described, parts of it, like plot and thoughts, are derived from *inventio*; its style, from *elocutio.*[45]

When Dryden shifts from the genius of the poet to the actual poem, he collapses the tripartite division into a dual one. The first two happinesses of the poet's imagination, illustrated by Ovid, make for the thoughts of a poem; the last happiness, of which Virgil is master, makes for elocution or style. Though both these poets give us lively and apt descriptions, Ovid's "wit written" is the result of the force of the imagination, whereas Virgil's is the effect of labor as well (16: 2). Ovid's is suited to drama in that, since the nature he describes is one of disorder, the words describing that nature must not admit "too curious an election," too

[44] Cf. R. S. Crane, "Neo-classical English Criticism," *Dictionary of World Literature,* ed. Joseph T. Shipley (New York, 1943), pp. 193-203.
[45] Cf. Dryden's *Parallel of Poetry and Painting,* where, in a context of art, rather than of the work of art, these three terms are made common to both poetry and painting: Invention (Ker, *op. cit.,* II, 138), Design (II, 140), and Cromatic, i. e. coloring in painting and expression in poetry (II, 147).

many tropes, or anything in the writing which carries the attention of the reader away from the object and closer to qualities in the poet's mind. In the sense of lively and apt, Ovid's writing is natural to drama; and in view of the later quarrel with Howard, to whom all this is written, it is significant that Dryden protects himself from admitting that the rimed couplet is unnatural to drama.

Since *Annus Mirabilis* is a historical poem (it is a political argument as well) and not a play, Dryden spends more time describing its elocution. In this Virgilian art the poet has the liberty to free himself from the object and to express his own soul: "We see the soul of the poet, like the universal one of which he speaks, informing and moving through all his [Virgil's] pictures" (16: 16-18). The main problem is still the appropriateness of words to thoughts. The thoughts of historical or heroic poetry differ from those of drama in that the poet is speaking through his own person rather than through the persons of the play. This gives the poet the liberty — so important in a later essay by Dryden on the very subject, the preface to *The State of Innocence* (1677) — of using metaphors and other tropes. Hence Dryden's account of his endeavors in the writing of *Annus Mirabilis* cannot end until he shows how, in this regard, he has attempted to imitate not Ovid but Virgil (17: 14 ff.). His premise, that it is fitting to use tropes and to adapt words freely, is based on the authority of Horace's precepts and Virgil's example. The entire argument rests on the appropriateness of the words to the thought and to the kind of poem, and to the poet's intention. Thus the "Verses to the Duchess" are no digression but an illustration of his argument (19: 10 ff.).

Dryden's answer to his question "How are the words of a poem to be made appropriate to its thoughts?" is this: Words are adapted to the subject as they are apt or exactly suited to the matter in hand and to the kind of poem, and as they are lively in allowing the soul of the poet to shine through them. The delight to be gained from this "elegant

adaptation " (to use a phrase coming much later) [46] presup-
poses a reader capable of feeling it. The preface, then, has
led to the solution of the problem. And it shows Dryden's
critical thinking from the outset to have its roots in the
rhetorical tradition of Horace and Quintilian. Literature is
judged by the criterion of nature imitated in a specified genre
and by the criterion of a particular audience who can recognize that nature and be pleased by it. Such an audience
would be made up of people more like Eugenius than like
Crites.

With this background we are in a better position to define
the problem of the *Essay of Dramatic Poesy* itself and the
method of Dryden's solution, remembering that the whole
discourse is sceptical, a way of reasoning used by Socrates,
Plato, and all the academics of old.

[46] Ker, *op. cit.*, I, 190: 15, in Dryden's definition of wit at the end of " The
Author's Apology for Heroic Poetry and Poetic Licence " (1677). Cf. my article
" Dryden's Discovery of Boileau," *Modern Philology*, 14 (1947), 112-117.

CHAPTER II

THE ARGUMENT

*"A play ought to be, A just and lively
image of human nature"* (36: 5).

T HE *Essay* opens with a proem of the time and the place
at which the four friends hold their discussion, a proem
which has a logical connection with the whole. The day sig-
nalizes the victory of the English nation over the Dutch
fleet,[1] and from the outset the note of English patriotism is
important to the position which, in the argument to follow,
the English drama of the age of Shakespeare and the riming
skill of Dryden's contemporaries hold in the entire scheme.
After the four friends from their vantage point on the river
had listened to the triumphant sound of the English cannon,
Eugenius "was the first who congratulated to the rest that
happy omen of our Nation's victory" (29: 21-24).

By obvious association this naval victory brings up for
discussion the large number of bad poems that will inevitably be written to celebrate it. Crites pursues this theme of
bad poets against the more measured tones of Eugenius.
According to Crites, the bad poets outnumber the good
in this age. Eugenius has already pleaded for moderation
with a quotation from Cicero concerning a bad poet who
was rewarded on condition that he remain thereafter silent
(30: 28–31: 1). But Crites' carping is seconded by Lisi-

---

[1] June 3, 1665, when the Duke of York, the King's brother, overcame the
Dutch fleet off the coast of Suffolk. Dryden himself, in his " paper of verses "
to the Duchess, had been among those who had felt the urge to celebrate in
rime the victory of a year later.

deius, and these two throughout the *Essay* maintain their views against the English. They particularize two poets as being especially bad. But, as with the characters in the debate, who these poets are [2] is less important in this analysis than what each represents. The difference between them is that the first lacks judgment and the second lacks fancy. The first bad poet deals in clenches and Clevelandisms and the kind of wit that turns only on words; he is clownish, a *mauvais buffon*, a satirical writer whose efforts at satire hurt no one, but who yet should be punished for the malice of wishing to hurt. In style and in matter, therefore, the first bad poet lacks the judgment to be a good poet; his imitation is not a " just " one. The " other extremity of poetry . . . having had some advantage of education and converse, knows better than the other what a poet should be " (31: 23-25) , but his " style and matter are everywhere alike." He never disquiets the emotions of his readers; he is a leveller in poetry. His apparent simplicity is a blind to his lack of imagination (32: 7) ; he never penetrates life, but skims the surface always, like the swallows that now fly over Thames (32: 13) . His imitation of nature is not a " lively " one. Eugenius reminds the two cynics that these two poets are certainly read, though not (the four would agree) by those who prefer Virgil to all other poets. Hence the peculiar force of Crites' quotation of Virgil (33: 6) .

In modern poets these two lacks, one of judgment and the other of imagination, are opposed to the quality of poetry in the last age and in ancient times (33: 13-14) ; and Crites and Lisideius between them have made such a condemnation of modern poetry that an argument is certain to ensue. Crites starts it by saying of the modern writers: " . . . they neither rise to the dignity of the last age, nor to any of the Ancients: and we may cry out of the writers of this time, with more reason than Petronius of his, *Pace vestra liceat dixisse, primi*

---

[2] See W. P. Ker, *The Essays of John Dryden* (Oxford, 1926), I, 289, 291. It was conjectured by Malone that the first poet may be Robert Wild, whose *Iter Boreale* was published in 1660, and that the second may be Richard Flecknoe. Evidence that Wild is one may be 32: 29; but Scott's conjecture of Samuel Holland for the second has as much ground as Malone's conjecture. Their poetic function within the " play " here is more significant.

omnium eloquentiam perdidistis:[3] you have debauched the true old poetry so far, that Nature, which is the soul of it, is not in any of your writings" (33: 13-19). Thus is introduced the "essay," whose very title, in its seventeenth-century meaning of testing the nature and excellence of a thing, gives the problem to be solved. Crites' condemnation fixes its major divisions. Clearly there are three ages of poetry to be compared: that of the Ancients, the "last age," and the present age. Eugenius adds to the conflict of the ages the conflict of "my own country" versus (by implication) some other country, which we later see to be France. It appears that Dryden's major concern is to reduce to a method through an imagined debate the rules by which drama has been written. The real function of Eugenius' next speech (33: 20–34: 14) is to delimit that problem. He asks two specific questions: What kind of poesy shall we argue about? Will Crites defend the general cause of the Ancients against the Moderns or oppose any age of the Moderns against this age of ours? In reply, Crites would limit the discussion to dramatic poesy, and within that subject prove that the Ancients are superior to the Moderns and that the dramatists of the last age are superior to those of today.

This response by Crites surprises Eugenius (34: 21) because, although he can argue against the first proposition, he partially agrees with the second. Thus Dryden establishes a common ground in the age of Shakespeare and Jonson, and sets the stage for the "characters" of Shakespeare, Jonson, and Beaumont and Fletcher, and for the examen of *The Silent Woman* in the main part of the *Essay*. Eugenius comforts himself with the thought that, if Englishmen of this age must yield in drama, it will be to Englishmen (34: 28), and not to contemporary French, Italian, and Spanish dramatists (35: 6). But even if the Restoration poets must bow in drama to the Elizabethans, they excel in two other forms of poesy: namely, the epic and the lyric (34: 30-31), here characterized only in terms of style and versification. The function of this momentary boast, which clearly lies

---

[3] Petronius, *Satyricon*, 2: " By your leave, let me say that you were the first to lose that eloquence."

outside the confines of the argument as already drawn, is to anticipate a superiority of modern *writing* as distinguished from *contrivance* necessitated by drama.[4] In contrast with the two bad poets condemned in the proem, the poets mentioned here — Suckling, Waller, Denham, and Cowley (35: 2-5) — possess in golden mean both correctness and spirit. Suckling and Waller represent the lyric; Denham and Cowley, epic. Since, of these writers, Suckling was long dead and Cowley had just recently died,[5] it is Waller and Denham, "yet living" (35:14), who "first taught us to mould our thoughts into easy and significant words; to retrench the superfluities of expression, and to make our rime so properly a part of the verse, that it should never mislead the sense, but itself be led and governed by it" (35: 14-19). This judgment, which echoes Dryden's immediately preceding exposition of "wit written," helps to justify the third section of this *Essay*.

But the problem was "Who writ the best plays" (35: 23-24)? So Lisideius, who later upholds the contemporary French drama, appropriately calls for a definition of a play to guide their discussion. After some "modest denials," Lisideius himself yields to the others' insistence that he give his notion of what a play ought to be. It ought to be: "A just and lively image of human nature, representing its passions and humours, and the changes of fortune to which it is subject for the delight and instruction of mankind" (36: 5-8).

This definition is the key to the structure and the traits of the *Essay of Dramatic Poesy*.[6] It is that which can be

---

[4] Cf. the prologue to *Secret Love* (1668), penned soon after the publication of the *Essay*, wherein Dryden speaks of compounding his play of "wit," on the one hand, and of "plot," on the other:

> " But while dead colours he with care did lay,
> He fears his wit, or plot, he did not weigh,
> Which are the living beauties of a play."
>   (Ker. *op. cit.*, I, 109).

[5] He died on July 28, 1667, according to A. H. Nethercot, *Abraham Cowley: The Muse's Hannibal* (London, 1931), p. 275. The evidence is the account in the London *Gazette* of August 4, 1667. Dryden's *Essay* was registered three days later.

[6] The finding of this definition in Corneille's *Discours* would give greater

taken for granted and so best conceded by all proponents.
We shall see how frequently all the speakers refer to its
various terms. Coming immediately after the statement of
the problem and its delimitation, it is the starting point from
which a solution of the problem can be reached. Everything
else in the *Essay* follows from it, and its removal would make
any assertions difficult to prove.

The terms in the definition are arranged in pairs and
within each pair are complementary one to the other. They
are the principles by which the problem is solved. These
dichotomous principles are: (1) a *just* and *lively* image of
human nature representing (2) its *passions* and *humours*
for tragedy and comedy and (3) its *passions and humours*
and *the changes of fortune* for characters and plot to the end
of (4) *delight* and *instruction.* The nature of Dryden's problem demands the use of complementary terms as principles
since the problem is one of opposing the plays of one age to
those of another in order to find a perfection. The first three
pairs are the traits in a play, or the means which implement
the end — the last pair. In arguing the excellence of plays,
both ancient and modern, the friends will have to use as
criteria these traits as the poet has used them to bring about
the end of drama. Hence the spheres of reference must be
(1) parts of the poem to be "essayed," that is, certain contrivances of drama and its writing; (2) the particular audiences, differing in geography and time, whether ancient,
French, or English; and (3) certain qualities in the genius of
the poet which emerge primarily in his style. The main device
of argument for a complete exploration of the problem must
be one of examples of plays, of the Ancients and the Moderns,
of the French and the English. And the most perfect plays
will be those whose parts please and instruct mankind
through being not only "just" (probable, true to life, exact

point to the statement that Dryden owes this essay to Corneille, but it is not
there. I have searched through a good deal of French criticism for a possible
source, but have not found it. A vague parallel is in " Discours de l'eloquence "
in *L'Art poétique de Colletet* (Paris, 1658), p. 18: "La poésie est une vive
représentation des choses naturelles." But there are doubtless hundreds of other
French or Italian sentences as close. Cf. René Bray, *La Formation de la doctrine
classique* (Paris, 1927), p. 18.

copies of nature), but also "lively" (heightened, effective, moving) representations of human nature.

Depending upon these principles and devices, the structure of the *Essay* demands three main parts, differentiated by the age. Each part is devoted to a pair of opponents speaking to the question: "Who has written the best plays according to the definition of a play?" These are (1) Crites, for the Ancients, and Eugenius, against the Ancients; (2) Lisideius, for the French, and Neander, for the English of the last age; and (3) Crites, against modern writing, and Neander, for present-day writing as excelling that of all challengers. The proportion of the first two parts to the last part is approximately that demanded by the temporary opposition of invention and disposition to elocution. The main protagonists, Crites and Neander, each speak twice. By making Crites uphold the Ancients and argue against contemporary writing and Neander uphold the age of Shakespeare as well as the style of Restoration poetry, Dryden succeeds in setting over the tripartite division the dual one of Ancients versus Moderns, as demanded early in the discussion by Crites (34:18-20). This dualism is adroitly furthered by making the French versus English argument in the central section go backwards. There time is stretched out from the French dramatists under Richelieu and almost up to the present *back* to the English flowering under Elizabeth and James.

To return to the text at the point of the definition of a play, Crites objects on logical grounds[7] to the definition as being one of genus and end. It is purposefully not specific enough. Epic will come under the same genus (101:26), and a plea for that kind of writing in heroic couplets which the dramatists contemporary with the speakers use in heroic plays will have a place in the argument about "who writ the best plays." But, the definition having been accepted, Crites starts out to prove by it that the Ancients are superior in dramatic poesy to the Moderns. Eugenius will attempt to show wherein Crites' argument is incomplete.

[7] Cf. the "Horatian definition" of satire in *Discourse concerning the Original and Progress of Satire*, Ker, *op. cit.*, II, 100-101.

I

Crites bases his argument for the Ancients on the well-known view of history that in the cycle of the Ancients the arts were born, flourished, and died. He argues a priori from cause to effect; if an age has a genius for a certain art or science, then that age will bring that art or science to perfection. Moderns, Crites continues, have a genius for science, rather than for art, and during the contemporary cycle of history the virtuosi have revealed "almost a new Nature" (36: 34–37: 1). Eugenius will hardly fail to use this opening in his rebuttal, for if the sciences have furthered knowledge of nature, then poesy, too, may improve with similar industry (44: 7–10). Crites continues: The age of art being past, the age of emulating fine artists is also passed. In any age in which emulation quickens endeavor, the art to which that endeavor is directed will be improved. This argument also goes from cause to effect, the causes being absent (emulation, esteem, rewards), the effect (fine plays) is also absent. In the place of emulation, Crites avers, is malice, and today we have few good poets but many severe judges (38: 1).

Crites has taken much of his discourse from Velleius Paterculus, *History of the Romans*, I, 16-17. From that work, as Malone notes, Dryden got his idea of the "universal genius" inhabiting every age, and certainly the quotation by Crites of Velleius' dictum concerning emulation as "the spur of wit"[5] is proof that Dryden either quoted from memory or had this work or a collection of *sententiae* from it before him. Of greater significance, however, than the use of this source for Crites' argument is the assumption that a failure to imitate the Ancients is a cause of our having so "few good poets" (38: 1). Passing from the poet to the poem, Crites attempts to prove this assumption by showing what it is in ancient plays that might profit the Moderns. His narrowness

[5] "Alit aemulatio ingenia ...." C. Velleius Paterculus, *Historiae Romanae*, I, 17, 6; ed. F. W. Shipley, Loeb Classical Library (London and New York, 1924), pp. 44-45. I have also consulted the English translation by J. S. Watson (Bohn).

of view is obvious, however, in his limiting the parts of a play to those which make more for a "just" image than for both a "just and lively" one: "Those Ancients have been faithful imitators and wise observers of that Nature which is so torn and ill represented in our plays; they have handed down to us a perfect resemblance of her" (38: 5-9). More specifically, the Ancients derived from their plays, Crites tells us, two kinds of rules for the writing of drama (a division of rules which Dryden had anticipated in the epistle on *Annus Mirabilis*): those rules which "relate to the justness and symmetry of the plot," and those which relate to "the episodical ornaments, such as descriptions, narrations, and other beauties, which are not essential to the play" (38: 15-17). The principle of this division gives the reason for the order in which the two kinds of rules are taken up, with certain enlargements, by each of the four speakers. For Crites, then, the ancient drama is superior in that, these rules having been observed by Aristotle and Horace from ancient drama, the traits in the play which they govern must then exist in the ancient drama.

As examples of the first kind of rules, those which make for "justness and symmetry of plot," Crites discusses "the famous Rules, which the French call Des Trois Unitez" (38: 28-29). This is Dryden's first mention of Corneille's three discourses, which, it was noted, many have recognized as a source of this essay. Merely to cite parallels of a French source, however, is unilluminating. Rather, one should first relate Dryden's use of the material at this point to its function in the solution of his problem; and then state and explain his divergence from Corneille.

The dramatic unities enter here as a means to Dryden's end in at least these three ways: (1) the unities are contrivances which govern the "changes of fortune" rather than the "passions and humours" of the definition; (2) as such they almost invariably make for a "just" rather than for a "lively" representation; and (3) as formulae which relate this "just image" to the ends of dramatic poesy, they have more to do with "instruction" than with "delight."[9]

[9] No whole but only half of the "just and lively" dichotomy is Crites' praise

As Crites limits himself only to plot here, Eugenius will answer him by stressing what Crites summarily dismisses as the "non-essential" parts of the play, by emphasizing the means of securing liveliness as well as justness to bring about delight as well as instruction. Crites only shows that the Ancients are superior to the Moderns because from them Aristotle and his followers arrived at the three unities "which ought to be preserved in every regular play" (38: 30-31), which is no more than saying that a play that does not observe them is irregular. Also, Crites subordinates the poet and the poem to the art of poetry by accounting for the rules as "nature methodiz'd," that is, necessary reconciliations between art and nature.

The first rule, the unity of Time, is upheld by Crites as making a play, as far as its plot or action is concerned, "the nearest [i.e. most just] imitation of nature" (39: 6-7). This rule of time is clearly set forth by Crites as a formula which relates the imagined or fictitious time of the action to the actual time of the performance. Fictionally, the time of a fable could be any number of hours; actually, the performance may require three hours. The rule of twenty-four hours — "the compass of a natural day" (38: 33) — is that which is contrived by the Ancients as a convenient reconciliation for the purpose of achieving "the nearest imitation of nature" (39: 2, 6). The same proportion of whole time to play should also obtain in each act (39: 9). Crites' mention of acts here will give his opponent an opening, as the Ancients did not divide their plays into acts. Finally, in order to get the action within these limits of time, the Ancients, Crites says, put some of their incidents into narrations (39: 27).

By the second rule, the unity of Place (the reason for this order of the three unities will soon be apparent), the Ancients intended that the scenes represented by the play be as few and as close together as possible. This likewise is a contrivance mainly for securing a just imitation. The stage being one place, it is unnatural (40: 5) to conceive of it as

---

of the Ancients, quoted above, as "faithful imitators" and "wise observers" of nature (38: 6).

many places, and the nearer those various places are, if it is so conceived, the better will the reason of the audience be beguiled. Hence the Ancients never changed the scene in the middle of an act, and they kept the audience aware of the sameness of place by never allowing the stage to be empty of characters. This is what Corneille called *la liaison des scènes* (40: 27).[10] "'Tis a good mark of a well-contrived play," Crites asserts, in speaking of how well the French have followed the Ancients in this regard. Crites had introduced the three unities as contrivances for both the justness and the symmetry of the plot; the rules themselves secure the justness, whereas the proportion of time between acts (in the first rule) and the *liaison des scènes* (in the second) help to secure the "symmetry" of the plot.

Finally, under "contrivance" Crites upholds the ancient drama in that it illustrates the unity of Action. This, he tells us, is what the logicians mean by *finis*, the end or scope of any action (40: 34); all other things in the play are to be made subservient to this "one great and complete action" (41:2-3). Crites' example from Terence's *Eunuch* makes the reconciling function of this rule clear: the main action is the marriage of Chaerea and Pamphila, and seeing it completed "leaves the mind of the audience in full repose" (41: 20). But complementary to this satisfaction of the judgment of the audience is its desire to have its imagination stimulated; hence that which secures "suspense of the imagination" is the secondary plot, the quarrel and reconciliation between two other lovers in the play that promotes the main business—the marriage of Chaerea and Pamphila (41: 16). The rule reconciles these two psychological reactions in the audience watching the play.

Unquestionably Dryden received from Corneille what he here puts into the mouth of Crites. There are many parallels. And, as we shall see in the next chapter (which distinguishes between what Dryden thought about the unities and what he made Crites think about them), his attitude of looking upon the unities as only a means to an end is that of Cor-

---

[10] Ker, *op. cit.*, I, 293; Pierre Corneille, *Œuvres*, ed. Charles Marty-Laveaux, 12 vols. (Paris, 1862), I, 101-102.

neille. But though the Frenchman takes up the unities in
the order of Action, Time, and Place, Dryden has Crites
discuss them in the order of Time, Place, and Action. Crites
is demonstrating that the Ancients, because their plays furnished that which led to the formulation of the rules, wrote
the better plays. He goes from the simplest one, that of
Time, to the most complicated, that of Action. Also, he
begins with those rules which are most likely to be disputed
by his opponents, and ends with his strongest argument,
with that rule which is least likely to be called in question.
For though Eugenius finds examples of the breaking of the
first two rules in plays of the Ancients, and asserts that they
did not discover the rule of Place, not one of the other speakers disputes what Crites says of the unity of Action. The reason for this is that, since Crites is speaking to the definition of
a play, though the first two rules may bring about a just imitation, it is the rule of Action that not only " leaves the mind
of the audience in a full repose," but also, by making the
lesser action subservient to the main one, holds the audience
" in a delightful suspense of what will be " (41: 20-23) . The
definition demanded that a good play be " just and lively."

   Crites has demonstrated that the Ancients made their
plays better in " contrivance " than the Moderns. He now
passes to their excellence in " writing " (41: 33) , a broad
term in his proposition (38: 10-23) which complements
" contrivance." The dialectic follows in general Quintilian's
" invention and arrangement " on the one hand, and his
" elocution " on the other. To make good the inference that
the Ancients " wrote better " (41: 33-34) , Crites argues as
follows. Much of their writing is lost, but there is ample
testimony of its high quality; if we had these lost pieces, the
controversy would be settled in the Ancients' favor (42:
1-10) . But we do have the comedies of Aristophanes and
of Plautus, and the tragedies of Euripides, Sophocles, and
Seneca — the first division of dramatic poesy into these two
genres. A comparison of the styles of these extant plays with
those of modern plays compels a greater admiration of the
Ancients (42: 10-15) . If we could understand them better
than we do, that admiration would be increased. Lack of

historical perspective keeps us from fully appreciating the
"propriety and elegancy" of Virgil's style (42: 23), terms
which parallel the "just and lively" of the definition (42:
15-30). Crites caps his argument by asserting that Ben
Jonson, who did understand the Ancients' writing, became a
learned plagiary of their style (42: 30 ff.).

The praise of Jonson, a favorite of Eugenius, is a delightful transition to the next speaker, who has all this time been
planning his answer. Crites had so continually emphasized
the just imitation of nature (though he has some of the lively,
too) that Eugenius will in all probability have to emphasize
the lack of liveliness. Again, although Crites based the
superiority of the Ancients upon their contrivance and writing, yet under the first he left a loophole for Eugenius by
failing to mention how regularly the Ancients observed the
rules which they discovered.

The function of Eugenius' answer, therefore, is to point
out some of the defects of the Ancients which Crites over-
looked and some of the excellencies of the Moderns (44:
14-15), according to the accepted standard proposed by
Lisideius. Since the main purpose is rebuttal, the beginnings
of the arguments of the first two opponents are alike. Crites
argued from cause to effect — the conditions being perfect,
the Ancient drama was perfect. Eugenius argues similarly
from a new cause—an even greater perfection of conditions.
The Moderns accept with gratitude the advantages derived
from the experience of the Ancients; Eugenius admits Crites'
point that all we know of the rules of this art comes from
them. But to this advantage we Moderns have added our
own industry in imitating nature itself: "We draw not therefore after their lines, but those of Nature; and having the
life before us, besides the experience of all they knew, it is
no wonder if we hit some airs and features which they have
missed" (43: 33–44: 4). Crites had already said that "nothing spreads more fast than science, when rightly and gen-
erally cultivated" (37: 6-7). If industry has made for progress in science today, Eugenius asserts, then it may — "with
the same pains" (44: 10) — make for progress in the other
arts, including poesy; consequently, Crites has failed to prove

that the Ancients made "more perfect images of human life than we" (44: 12). But though Eugenius announces his double intention of refuting Crites and adding "some few excellencies" of the Moderns, actually he fails to complete his second intention. The result is that his function is to round out Crites' arguments for the Ancients, thus opening up the way for Lisideius to expand the definition of a play with examples from modern French, and for Neander with examples from the English of the last age and of this.

Eugenius corrects and expands Crites' views by stressing those parts of a play which are not "writing" in far more general terms than Crites' "contrivance." By distinguishing between the laying of the plot (*inventio*) and the managing of the plot (*dispositio*) he adds to the parts of a play the characters that depend upon the plot. And he expands writing to include the thoughts or movements of the mind, which become the "passions" of the definition scarcely touched upon by Crites. Throughout, as Crites showed the images of the Ancients to be mainly just, Eugenius proves that they were not always lively.

Eugenius' first purpose being to "show you some part of their defects" (44: 14), he begins with the most general and goes on to the more specific. The Ancients, in the first place, had not "arrived to perfection" (44: 27), as Crites had said they had, because they did not know how to divide a play into acts. Writing by entrances instead of by acts, they had "rather a general indigested notion of a play, than knowing how and where to bestow the particular graces of it" (45: 31–46:2). Scaliger (Dryden says Aristotle), indeed, had divided a play into four integral parts: the protasis, epitasis, catastasis, and catastrophe (44:35). Thus "Aristotle" gave us an "image of a play . . . so lively, that from thence much light has been derived to the forming it more perfectly into acts and scenes" (45: 22-25). But the ancient dramatists did not so divide their plots. Though there is no necessity for five acts, some plan or principle is preferable to chance (46: 11).

More specific are the Ancients' failures in plot. Eugenius divides these into "laying of the plot," which includes the

characters, and "managing the plot" (50: 9-10), under which
he takes up their lack of regularity in applying the three
dramatic unities. As for "laying of the plot," the Ancients
ill satisfied one end of dramatic poesy, that of delight. They
laid their plots on old stories, the outcome of which was
patent to the audiences: "the novelty being gone, the pleasure vanished; so that one main end of Dramatic Poesy in its
definition, which was to cause delight, was of consequence
destroyed" (47: 1-4). Crites himself had previously called
the element of suspense "delightful" (41: 22-23). But in
the Greek laying of plots there is no suspense (46: 31-35).
The Roman comic plots are as trite as those of Greek tragedy
(47: 5-15); and the whole absence of original invention
amounts, in Eugenius' argument, to a lack of liveliness.

The characters, too, are "indeed the imitations of Nature,
but so narrow, as if they had imitated only an eye or an
hand" (47: 33–48: 1); that is, according to the definition,
the characters of ancient comedy are, in a limited way only,
a just image, and certainly not a lively one.

Eugenius' division in the plotting parallels invention and
disposition. At this point he passes to "managing of the
plots": "But in how strait a compass soever they have
bounded their plots and characters, we will pass it by, if they
have regularly pursued them, and perfectly observed those
three Unities of Time, Place, and Action" (48: 4-7). Eugenius is still pointing out defects in the treatment of the
"changes of fortune," rather than in the "passions and
humours." As the first part of his strictures on ancient
plotting showed a lack of liveliness (plots and characters in
too strait a compass), so the managing of those plots is de-
fective in that it made the plays of the Ancients less just.
The lack of regularity is a dissatisfaction that comes from a
lack of proportion. Crites had arranged the three unities in
order of Time, Place (under which came the liaison des
scènes), and Action. This order is momentarily disrupted by
Eugenius, who first mentions the unity of Place (48: 9-10).
But he is refuting Crites' assertion that the Ancients are
mainly to be admired for giving us the three dramatic unities; that of Place is a notorious exception, as Corneille said:

Quant à l'unité de lieu, je n'en trouve aucun précepte ni dans Aristote, ni dans Horace.[11]

. . . the Unity of Place, however it might be practised by them, was never any of their rules: we neither find it in Aristotle, Horace, or any who have written of it, till in our age the French poets first made it a precept of the stage (48: 10-14).

But in his actual discussion of the three unities, Dryden makes Eugenius follow the order of Crites, in spite of the fact that he is taking much of his material from Corneille's *Trois Discours*; yet his argument demands one important omission, that of the unity of Action, for reasons to be discussed. As Crites had done, Eugenius begins with the unity of Time (48: 7, 14). This unity the Ancients have failed to observe regularly in their "managing of plots," for many of them omit it entirely from their plays, and, if they do include it, they observe it so "narrowly" as to make for absurdities. Of this failure, Eugenius cites three examples: from Terence's *Self-Punisher*, from Euripides' *Suppliants*, and again from Terence's *Eunuch*. The first example Dryden took from Scaliger (48: 17). The second example Corneille uses (cf. 49: 2-4) to illustrate the ancient failure to observe the unity of Time:

Euripide, dans *les Suppliants*, fait partir Thésée d'Athènes avec une armée, donner une bataille devant les murs de Thèbes, qui en étoient éloignés de douze ou quinze lieues, et revenir victorieux en l'acte suivant; et depuis qu'il est parti jusqu'à l'arrivée du messager qui vient faire le récit de sa victoire, Éthra et le chœur n'ont que trente-six vers à dire. C'est assez bien employé [*sic*] un temps si court.[12]

Euripides, in tying himself to one day, has committed an absurdity never to be forgiven him, for in one of his tragedies he has made Theseus go from Athens to Thebes, which was about forty English miles, under the walls of it to give battle, and appear victorious in the next act; and yet from the time of his departure to the return of the Nuntius, who gives the relation of his victory, Æthra and the Chorus have but thirty-six verses; that is not for every mile a verse (48: 19-28).

[12] *Ibid.*, I, 112.   [11] Ker, *op. cit.*, I, 117.

Under the unity of Place — that being the anticipated order—Eugenius, like Crites, includes the *liaison des scènes* (49: 7), which he grants the Ancients to have kept better; but he insists that the reason for it is the paucity and brevity of their scenes (another example of the lack of " liveliness "). Both the idea and the example from the third act of Terence's *Eunuch* Dryden took from Corneille's third discourse:

Les anciens ne s'y sont pas toujours assujettis, bien que la plupart de leurs actes ne soient chargés que de deux ou trois scènes; ce qui la rendoit bien plus facile pour eux que pour nous, qui leur en donnons, quelque fois jusqu'à neuf ou dix, [Here one example is given from Sophocles' *Ajax*] . . . l'autre [exemple] est du troisième acte de *l'Eunuque* de Térence, où celle d'Antiphon seul n'a aucune communication avec Chrémès et Pythias, qui sortent du théâtre quand il y entre.[13]	. . . but the reason is, because they have seldom above two or three scenes, properly so called, in every act . . . . Now the plots of their plays being narrow, and the persons few, one of their acts was written in a less compass than one of our well wrought scenes; and yet they are often deficient even in this. To go no further than Terence, you find in the *Eunuch* Antipho entering single in the midst of the third act, after Cremes and Pythias were gone off . . . (49: 12-23).

Yet Terence often breaks the *liaison des scènes,* using " the unnatural way of narration " (50: 3).

Up to this point Eugenius has shown how the Ancients have failed in those traits of a play which give delight to the audience; so, also according to the definition of a play, they have failed in instruction, as Eugenius proves by citing examples of a lack of poetic justice (50: 15-23).

After the unity of Time and of Place one would expect Eugenius to take up the unity of Action, but he leaves Crites' assertions (41: 7 ff.) in regard to Action totally unanswered. However dull their plots, the Ancients were not so vulnerable in this unity as in the other two unities. Because he failed to show how the Moderns have profited from the Ancients, the third speaker, Lisideius, will demonstrate his conception of the perfect play by citing examples of the unity of Action in French drama.

Instead of taking up the unity of Action, Eugenius,

[13] *Ibid.,* I, 101-102.

anxious to show the defects of the Ancients, asserts that among them no one man wrote both tragedy and comedy, but "he who found his genius bending to the one, never attempted the other way" (50: 26-28). This is a shift from the work to the artist. Eugenius is making a transition from the plots and characters of the Ancients' plays to their writing, that is, from *inventio* and *dispositio* to *elocutio*. Up to this point he has spoken of the classical plays as "swerving from nature" and failing thereby to please the audience; with his transition to the writing he adds another sphere of reference, the genius of the poet, which, with "correctness" —an appeal to the properly cultivated audience—is Dryden's usual criterion for style.

The few excellencies of the Moderns (44: 15) which Eugenius promised to discuss consist mainly of the Moderns' ability to recognize the wit (51: 1) of the Ancients, contrary to Crites' assertion. Here again Eugenius does not oppose the writing of modern plays to the writing of ancient plays, nor does he correct what Crites had said of ancient writing; but he expands Crites' conception of the perfect writing of a play. He first answers his opponent's warning about not being too ready to judge wit, by insisting upon its universal character. One couplet in Cleveland, even, is "wit in all languages" — if it is "a thing well said" (51: 7-8 and 53: 1). With this distinction between the "thing" and the "well saying," Eugenius builds upon Crites' foundation of the elocution of a perfect play. As for the "well saying," a general rule is made negatively; the poet should neither coin new words nor be too bold in his metaphors. These liberties are opposed to the kind of language which, as Horace tells, is not new-coined but accepted by custom, and which is not bold but easy (51: 31). In the Roman tongue, Plautus is an example of the new-coining stylist, and Terence of the opposite. In English, the opposition is illustrated on one side by the satirist Cleveland, whose "express[ing of] a thing hard and unnaturally, is his new way of elocution" (52: 2-3). Virgil and Ovid have used catachreses with judgment, but to use them too often is bad.

As for the "thing" which is thus "well said," Eugenius

repeats that wit "is most to be admired when a great thought comes dressed in words so commonly received, that it is understood by the meanest apprehensions" (52: 21-22). This is an appeal to the best audience as identified with the common sense of posterity. As before he divided the "well saying" into "easy language" and the "coining of words and the use of bold metaphors," so now he couples the "language" to the "thought." The thought and the well saying of it must be suited one to the other, as in Dryden's *Annus Mirabilis.* An example of the imperfect joining of these two is Cleveland, an English wit who has "common thoughts in abstruse words." His style is opposed to that of Donne, who "gives us deep thoughts in common language" (52: 29-32). As for Roman poets, Seneca has "excellent thoughts" (53: 12), but Ovid, who best combines "thoughts" and the "easy language" appropriate to them, is the "genius most proper for the stage" (53: 13-14). With Ovid, Eugenius passes to the "passions" as the "thing" in dramatic wit which is to be "well said." Thus in Eugenius' dialectic the "thing" has shifted to the "thought," which in turn has become the "passions." The passions are the "various movements of the soul," as opposed to "changes of fortune": ". . . the audience . . . watch the movements of their [the characters'] minds, as much as the changes of their fortunes. For the imaging of the first is properly the work of a poet; the latter he borrows of the historian" (54: 27-31).

Thus Eugenius has not refuted Crites on the ancient wit. Nor has he particularly upheld, against Crites, the superiority of modern wit. In some modern poets he has actually condemned it. In adding many more distinctions to wit, however, he has emphasized delight and liveliness by relating wit to the genius of the poet who writes it. Whereas Crites devoted only about half of his speech to wit, Eugenius gives about two thirds to this element in a play. Also, in the relationship here between the thought and the word lies the germ of Dryden's later definition of wit as propriety (190: 11-16).

At this point Crites, interrupting (54: 32), remarks that the Moderns have not arrived at a better "image of nature" but have merely altered the method of arriving at it. Insist-

ing upon his original position of cause in the spirit of the age
as having an effect in drama, he does not give up his view
that the Ancients, living in a better time, wrote better plays.
Aptly quoting from Horace (55: 19) — had Lucilius been
forced by fate to be born in this day, he would accommodate
himself to the new habits of writing [14] — Crites temporarily
reconciles the dispute, though Eugenius "seemed to have
the better of the argument" (55: 30) .[15]

This ends the first part of the *Essay*. The argument of
the first two speakers has a cumulative effect which lends
elements of form to the unity of the whole. The essay
obviously is synthetic, not analytic; each of these first
speakers starts with a definition purposely framed in universal terms and adds to the concept of a perfect play.
Eugenius accepts Crites' proposal that the Moderns have
profited from the rules of the Ancients. The movement has
been from nature to art, and there has not been a clear distinction between these two universal terms. Under art, both
speakers have kept within the two broad parts of the play—
contrivance and writing. Their principles have a tendency
to fall into pairs of complementary terms. As for the excel-
lency of ancient plays, the second speaker grants their superiority in contrivance, by means of which the rules of dramatic
unity have been justified. But a superiority in other dramatic
elements besides plot has been anticipated for the Moderns.

II

The next section carries on the discussion. Here the two
new opponents, Lisideius and Neander, argue respectively
for the French and for the English as the makers of the perfect play. Aside from its connection with the whole — particularly the "just" and "lively" opposition — the third
speaker's discourse is specifically anticipated by two failures

---

[14] *Satires*, I, 10, 68; cf. Ker, *op. cit.*, I, 163: 20.
[15] The principle of relativity used by Crites, which became popular in the
eighteenth century and culminated in Taine, is not common in Dryden's time.
An even better example comes later in the *Essay* (72: 5-12) in the argument
concerning the difference between French and English plays as being due to the
differing national temperaments of the two peoples.

of Eugenius. Eugenius had said, "as for the Italian, French, and Spanish plays, I can make it evident, that those who now write surpass them; and that the Drama is wholly ours" (35: 5-8). But he did not fulfill this promise. Moreover, of his own intentions in arguing against Crites, he had only partially fulfilled the second: to show how modern plays are superior. Lisideius acknowledges himself to be of the same opinion of the Ancients, but among the Moderns why does Eugenius prefer the English to other nations, particularly to the French, noted for their exactness (56: 4)?

Lisideius then launches into a defence, not of the justness or exactness for which the French are so well known, but of the way in which the French make plot the means to the end of moving an audience. After granting that forty years ago English drama had been superior to the French of that time, he asks whether any nation *in this age* better observes the rules of the Ancients than the French (57: 3). Because Crites spoke of the Ancients' invention of the three unities and Eugenius pointed out how the Ancients had failed to comply with the first two of them, Lisideius has a logical opening to show in what the modern French excel, that is, in observing the rules better than the modern English and Spanish do. Taking up the rules, in the same order, he dismisses the unity of Time and the unity of Place in a few lines (57: 3-15) in order to concentrate upon the unity of Action, which Eugenius had entirely omitted.

The arguments Lisideius adduces to prove the French superior in their plays are arranged according to these parts of a play: the plot (57: 16-61: 5), the characters (61: 10-35), the thoughts and words as they exist in the narrations of these characters (62: 4-32), and the beauty of French rime (67: 6-25). He adds new distinctions to all of these, and also makes certain omissions. But mainly he treats the parts of a play as the means to the end of eliciting an emotional reaction from the audience. He sets delight and liveliness, in the definition of a play, above instruction and justness.

By keeping within the rule of unity of Action the modern French dramatists have given us a hallmark of French tragedy: their plots are single, not burdened with underplots.

A double action is censured for interfering with the "concernment" of the audience (57: 23-26). This allows Lisideius to condemn the English tragicomedy on the grounds that mirth and compassion, mingled together, cancel each other, and lead to the absurdities of the English. A double plot deprives a serious play of the accomplishment of its main end, which is to "beget admiration, compassion, or concernment" (58: 10). The French attain this end without sacrificing variety (58: 3). Later on Neander refutes this by distinguishing between the thing itself and the manner of doing the thing (69: 24).

Another advantage in plot, besides that derived from the unity of Action, is that French plots are often based on some well-known incident of history. Here the Moderns have imitated the Ancients, and surpassed them. By weaving truth with this "probable fiction," the French plot makers have achieved far greater suspense, and thus French drama has more emotional appeal to an audience than does the ancient drama. Still keeping within the bounds of probability, the French dramatist "dispenses with the severity of history" (59: 2). Thus his manner of treating history is not only just but lively as well. With this just and lively historical plotting of the French, Lisideius contemptuously compares the plotting of the chronicle plays of Shakespeare, which (to borrow a metaphor from Corneille) [16] is "to look upon . . . [Nature] through the wrong end of a perspective" (59: 23-24), and thus fail to attain the end of delight (59: 26).

A third difference between the modern French and English plotting (59: 33) — derived from the unity of Action — is that the French do not encumber their single plots with so many turns, complexities of episodic material, as do the Spanish in their complicated plots. Through this simplicity of plot construction the French "have gained more liberty for verse," and they have more leisure to "represent the passions," acknowledged in the definition of a play to be the poet's work (60: 11-14). Lisideius omits the "humours,"

[16] *Œuvres* (1862), I. 113; cf. Pierre Legouis, " Corneille and Dryden as Dramatic Critics," *Seventeenth Century Studies Presented to Sir Herbert Grierson* (Oxford, 1938), p. 283.

equally vital to the foundation of the argument, because he is confining himself to tragedy. The element of humours in the definition will be expanded by Neander's examen of Jonson. Of the English tragedies only one, *Rollo*, Lisideius argues, has some claim to this simplicity of plot; but Jonson's *Sejanus* and *Catiline* are "unnatural mixture[s] of comedy and tragedy." The tragic incidents grow out of the single plot, but the comic episodes seem of "an ill mingle with the rest" (61:5) — a challenge to Neander.

Necessary to the disposition of the single plot is one main character (and here Lisideius passes to another element of the play), for by concentrating on this character the poet can "pursue close" his "one argument." Lisideius upholds the single main character by an analogy with the state — a single ruler with all other people subservient to him. The other characters cannot be unnecessary in so nice a balance, for they either help to carry the plot or help the audience to understand it (61:32-33). The characters of the latter function can speak the lines which convey related action. The French usually make them actual agents in the action, rather than extra persons brought in for no other reason than to give reports (62:1-4).

This brings Lisideius to the next element of a play, the speeches, which are compounded of thoughts and words and yet spring from the action. Here Dryden, following Corneille, makes Lisideius distinguish between two kinds of narrations: those which give antecedent action or exposition and those concerned with "things happening in the action of the play" (62:22). By concentrating on this latter type of narration, again the French — through this contrivance — gain certain advantages: they avoid the ridiculous unjustness of the English attempts to portray duels, army maneuvers, and death scenes on the stage; and thereby the French have freer rein for the depiction of the passions.[17] Through words the poet not only describes nature but heightens it: 'All *passions*

---

[17] Pierre Legouis, *op. cit.*, p. 285, sees a parallel here to *Œuvres* (1862), I, 104-105: "j'ajoute un conseil," etc., but he notes that Dryden's comparisons are original.

may be lively represented on the stage . . . , but there are
many *actions* which can never be imitated to a just height"
(63:3-8). Thus the French dramatists make good plays,
Lisideius argues, in that by the use of narration to arouse
concernment their "images of human nature" include the
passions as part of the action (64:17-22). To anticipate
possible criticism on this point from Neander, Lisideius gives
examples of the narrating of action in English plays by
Jonson and Fletcher to prove that it is not the thing which
is to be condemned but the way of doing the thing (65:
30-32). Neander will turn this about for tragicomedy.

Two other advantages which the French have over the
English Lisideius passes over with mere mention. One is an
additional excellence of plot, which is more the justness than
the liveliness of the definition (Lisideius has been emphasizing the latter); that is, the French avoid ending plays
with a conversion or a simple change of will (66:1-22). In
this respect they are "just" without being dull, and hence
surpass the Ancients. Again, the French insist that all entrances and exits of characters be for a manifest reason
(66:23–67:5).[18]

Up to this point Lisideius has argued that the French
excel the English in such contrivances as plotting, making
the characters unify the plot, and narrating certain incidents
in order better to portray the passions: "I should now speak
of the beauty of their rhyme, and the just reason I have to
prefer that way of writing in tragedies before ours in blank
verse" (67:6-8). But he does not think it necessary to argue
this. He has already touched upon words in descriptions
(63:20). Furthermore, rime is "partly received by us";
and the only reason he sees why it is not more followed in
English tragedies is that "our poets write so ill in it" (67:
14)—the same argument that later Dryden uses against
his brother-in-law. When good English poets speak against
rime, Lisideius is troubled. But for the bad poets who decry

---

[18] Corneille, *Œuvres* (1862), I, 108: ". . . il n'y a rien de si mauvaise grâce
qu'un acteur qui se retire du théâtre seulement parce qu'il n'a plus de vers à
dire." Cf. Legouis, *op. cit.*, p. 286; Dorothy Burrows, "The Relation of Dryden's
Serious Plays and Dramatic Criticism to Contemporary French Literature"
(doctoral dissertation, University of Illinois, 1933), p. 75.

rime he has a quotation from Velleius Paterculus, the meaning of which is that, despairing of outdoing those whom we
consider foremost, we decline to follow them in their excellence and, instead, seek something else in which to excel—
"praeteritoque eo in quo eminere non possumus, aliquid in
quo nitamur conquirimus" (67:24-25).[19]   Just what that
aliquid is in which the modern English dramatists can hope
to excel both the Ancients and the French will be explained
by the next speaker, Neander (cf. 99:16-20).

Neander's arguments, the main part of the essay, will
give us for the first time a perfectly explicit laying out of all
the sets of contraries in the definition, which is the basis of
the argument concerning the ideal play. Neander will show
that the English drama is superior to all because it is a lively
and just imitation of the humours and passions as well as
the changes of fortune of human nature, for the end of delight
and instruction. In his "To the Reader," Dryden had
written: "The drift of the ensuing Discourse was chiefly to
vindicate the honour of our English writers, from the censure
of those who unjustly prefer the French before them" (27:
12-15).

But before we explain Neander's real contribution to the
expansion of the definition of a play, we shall have to see
what he acknowledges from his predecessors in the argument,
and then dispose of his rebuttal. "I shall grant Lisideius,"
he says, "without much dispute, a great part of what he has
urged against us; for I acknowledge that the French contrive
their plots more regularly, and observe the laws of comedy,
and decorum of the stage ι . . . with more exactness than the
English" (67:28-33). The purpose of his rebuttal is to show
that the virtues of the French and the faults of the English
which Lisideius may have brought out are virtues and faults
of plot, that part of a play which mainly concerns the
"changes of fortune." In his initial speech, then, Neander
first refutes Lisideius' arguments that French contrivance in

---

[19] Velleius Paterculus, I, 17, 7 (Loeb Classical Library, pp. 46-47). Dryden
omits the preceding clause, "velut occupatam relinquens materiam, quaerit
novam," because his argument does not call for abandoning the ancient ground
but using as much of it as is still valid.

plot is the best means of liveliness (67: 28–78: 29); next, in
the positive part of his first speech—the three "characters"
and the examen (78: 30–89: 31)—he argues that other parts
of the play, besides plot, are further means to the whole end.

Though the French may be more regular and exact,
Neander insists that the French by that are not "above us,"
since their plays do not conform to the multiple requirements
of the definition:

> For the lively imitation of Nature being in the definition of a play,
> those which best fulfil that law ought to be esteemed superior to the
> others. 'Tis true, those beauties of the French poesy are such as will
> raise perfection higher where it is, but are not sufficient to give it where
> it is not: they are indeed the beauties of a statue, but not of a man,
> because not animated with the soul of Poesy, which is imitation of
> humour and passions (68: 2-11).

Here for the first time a new principle is brought into the
argument — not that a play must combine the "just and
lively" merely, but that "lively" is superior to "just."
A statue is an exact imitation of nature, but it is not alive.
Hence the soul of poesy, which for Aristotle is the plot, for
Dryden (speaking here partially through Neander?) is the
"imitation of humour and passions." The French *humeurs*
compared with the English humours of comedy are dead;
and so are the French serious characters when compared
with the English. Thus the French comedies, particularly,
lack the variety, the fullness, the live quality of Jonson's
Alchemist, Epicœne, and *Bartholomew Fair* (69: 15). And
at least in liveliness Shakespeare may be Jonson's superior
(cf. 79: 29-30). As though the French were aware of their
lack, since Richelieu's death their younger dramatists have
been mixing mirth and tragedy, a practice Lisideius over-
looked (69: 2-6). Although the French have made the Spanish plots more regular, it is not the theory but the practice
of the French in attempting tragicomedy that Neander con-
demns. The theory is good in that mirth and compassion
are not incompatible; the one sets off the other (70: 1).
Why should Lisideius have harped on the unity of Action in
French plays, Neander asks, the plots of which are barren
compared with the copiousness of the English (70: 16-19)?

The main plot, like the Primum Mobile, must be fashioned
to give the motion to the varidirectioned smaller planets
(70:25–71:12). It all depends upon how well the poet by
subordinating his lesser plot to the main design achieves
variety in addition to regularity. Neander's defense of tragicomedy, couched mainly in questions, is as sceptical as anything in Dryden's sceptical essay. Years later, however, in
the *Parallel of Poetry and Painting*, Dryden differed with
his Neander in considering the comic and serious parts of the
Spanish Friar: ". . . they are of an unnatural mingle: for
mirth and gravity destroy each other" (II, 147).

Lisideius had furnished only an English example for the
liberty which the unity of Action gives to represent the passions (60:11-20); now Neander challenges him to find a
French example (71:16). By their singleness of plot, rather,
the French had to introduce long speeches, which tire the
audience. There are national differences in audiences: the
French, a gay people, prefer tragedy; the English, "a more
sullen people," (72:7) prefer comedy. Here once more is the
relativist position which, by reducing the number of universal
rules, makes Dryden's *Essay* so much less of an *ipse dixit*
than is commonly supposed. Within the argument, the
appeal to national differences further prepares for the
supreme English contribution in contrivance—the humours
play, and the best example of it, Jonson's *Silent Woman*.
But Neander's argument is that English plays stir the passions better because the speeches are shorter, a rhetorical
consideration of drama. Shorter speeches, like those in actual
life, are more natural (72:15). As Neander is following the
order of argument in Lisideius' speech, this point closes the
section on plot.

Lisideius' next point was that the French had an advantage in making only one person the hero (61:10). Neander
admits that one character should be outstanding, but adds
that the more secondary persons there are the greater will
be the variety of plot (73:11). The English derive this unity
from a single main character, but possess an added richness
as in *The Maid's Tragedy, The Alchemist,* and *The Silent
Woman* (73:20). So much for Lisideius' "characters."

The next argument in favor of the French given by Lisideius was the *bienséance* which the French dramatists preserve through narrating certain actions rather than representing them (62: 4 ff.). Neander asks (74: 1 ff.) what criteria should be used for designating certain actions for narration. English tastes are more bloodthirsty than those of the French. Furthermore, Corneille's *Andromède* is seen to possess many an improbable action which is represented and not narrated. And yet Neander is willing to compromise: " To conclude on this subject of relations; if we are to be blamed for showing too much of the action, the French are as faulty for discovering too little of it: a mean betwixt both should be observed by every judicious writer, so as the audience may neither be left unsatisfied by not seeing what is beautiful, or shocked by beholding what is either incredible or undecent " (75: 14-21).

Lisideius had claimed two further advantages for French plotting: one having to do with conversions, and the other with entrances (66: 2 and 66: 23). But Neander hastens on to his actual plea for English drama. Up to this point he has argued "that though we are not altogether so punctual as the French, in observing the laws of Comedy, yet our errors are so few, and little, and those things wherein we excel them so considerable, that we ought of right to be preferred before them " (75: 23-27). Before presenting additional proof that " we excel them " in many things, he makes a fine point of adducing Corneille, Lisideius' main prop for French drama, as arguing against the excessive restriction of the French rules (75: 30 ff.). To illustrate the negative result of a too strict observance of the rules, Neander speaks only of the unities of Time and of Place, omitting here the unity of Action, since it is under that rule that he has refuted some of Lisideius' arguments and later will discuss tragicomedy. Lisideius had attempted to show how through the rules the French obtained probability, whereas Neander shows what ridiculous improbabilities often resulted through too strict an application of these two rules.[20]

[20] Legouis, *op. cit.*, p. 290, contends that Neander is being sophistical when he picks out an unrepresentative play by Corneille's younger brother (text, 76: 34).

And this leads him to ask the question which actually begins, once his rebuttal is finished, his defence of the English drama: "Now what, I beseech you, is more easy than to write a regular French play, or more difficult than write an irregular English one, like those of Fletcher, or of Shakespeare" (77: 20-23) ?

English drama is superior in those two general parts of the play which have been kept separate by all three speakers so far: namely, in contrivance and in wit, or writing, "For, if you consider the plots, our own are fuller in variety; if the writing, ours are more quick and fuller of spirit" (78: 1-3). Here again are the characteristic touchstones of Horace's and Quintilian's rhetorical approach: plot is a combination of *inventio* and *dispositio*, whereas *elocutio* governs style. In both these things English plays are thoroughly English; they have borrowed neither contrivance nor writing from any others. The very brief history of rime at this point is brought in to prove only that English spirit and variety are not copied from the French.

Returning from the digression (78: 30) on rime, Neander "boldly affirms" these two propositions of the English drama as growing out of the relationships already established between contrivance and wit: "First, that we have many plays of ours as regular as any of theirs, and which, besides, have more variety of plot and characters; and secondly, that in most of the irregular plays of Shakespeare or Fletcher (for Ben Jonson's are for the most part regular) there is a more masculine fancy and greater spirit in the writing, than there is in any of the French" (78: 32–79: 4). The term "writing of a play" is, then, far more general here than it has been in the previous distinction between contrivance and wit. But the term has already been introduced by Eugenius as one trait of a play whose criterion of excellence is to be found more in certain qualities of the poet's soul than in the satisfaction of the audience or mere verisimilitude. It would appear, therefore, that Neander's second proposition will demand an exploration into the meaning of "genius." Hence the characters of English dramatists asked for at this point (79: 17) serve at least two functions.

Since the second proposition clearly limits the field to the dramatists of the previous age, the characters of those two poets whose plays are not as regular as Jonson's become necessary, and their "masculine fancy and greater spirit in the writing" must be shown with reference to qualities of mind in the writers themselves. The examination of "writing" in the stricter sense will be reserved for the final argument (the third part of the *Essay*), that between Crites and Neander, and its scope will be shifted from the writing of the previous age to that of this age. The reason for taking up the "spirit in writing" first, and then the "regularity with variety," contrary to the announced order, is that Neander can end this part of his discourse with the most telling example of a play that is as just as any of the French plays his opponent has mentioned and yet much more lively.

Another function of the three characters is to give Neander's reasons for choosing Jonson's *Silent Woman* as the best English play to prove his first affirmation (78:32-34). To Shakespeare, "all images of Nature were still present" (79:34); he drew them luckily (80:1). Jonson, on the other hand, drew them "laboriously" (80:1). Shakespeare is the "greater wit" (82:31), whereas Jonson is "the more correct poet" (82:30. The purpose of the examen is to furnish proof that English plays are as just as those of the Ancients and the French, and at the same time—through the humours of the definition—as lively also. Shakespeare is the Homer, great but rugged; Jonson is the Virgil, the pattern of elaborate writing (82:33). Shakespeare came first — he is the father of English dramatic poesy (82:32). Jonson came after. By an implied law of progress, then, Jonson is the poet whose work will best bear comparison with that of the Ancients and of the French. Neander loves Shakespeare, but he admires Jonson (83:1); for love is natural affection, and admiration the result of a judiciously cultivated taste. Finally, Jonson has given us in his *Discoveries* rules for the stage as profitable as those of Corneille (83:3-5). In short, Jonson best combines the just and the lively, and so he is the best example for Neander's argument.

The three sets of characters themselves add certain terms

and relationships artistically and logically justified by the *Essay* as a whole. The characters are not simply put in here; and they cannot simply be taken out, as J. H. Smith takes them out of context for separate admiration.[21] They are part of the movement of the whole from nature to art. And it is this movement which prescribes their ordering: Shakespeare was "naturally learn'd" (80:4); Beaumont and Fletcher had "great natural gifts, improved by study" (86:28-29); and Jonson contributed "something of art [that] was wanting to the Drama, till he came" (82:2). Shakespeare had the greatest strength, in other words, but Jonson best managed his strength.

So far, then, Neander has expatiated upon the genius which makes for "greater spirit in the writing" and has justified his choosing as an example of the first assertion a play by Ben Jonson. He is ready to support that boast by an examen of Jonson's *The Silent Woman* (83:7). Since part of his purpose is to prove that this comedy is as true an imitation of nature as the plays of the Ancients and of the French, and observes as carefully the laws of comedy, Neander will dilate first upon its regularity, and then show how in that regularity there is variety. The first is just, the second lively; the first instructs the audience, the second delights it. For the rules he follows the order of Crites (38:32 ff.) and Lisideius (48:7): the unity of Time in *The Silent Woman* (83:10-16); the unity of Place, under which is discussed the *liaison des scènes* (83:16-24); and the unity of Action (83:24 ff.). This is regularity with a vengeance. Yet the dialectic of the whole shows clearly that in each pair of terms used one is of higher value than the other; liveliness is set above justness, and delight above instruction. Accordingly, observance of these laws of unity is only half of the image and in Dryden's view the less important half, since the Greeks and the French followed them very nicely, too. They make for a just image only.

That is why, next, Neander is made to concentrate on the variety of characters which Jonson has attained within

---

[21] John Harrington Smith, "Dryden's Critical Temper," *Washington University Studies*, Humanistic Series, 12, No. 2 (St. Louis, 1925), 201-220.

his single plot: " The intrigue of it is the greatest and most noble of any pure unmixed comedy in any language; you see in it many persons of various characters and humours, and all delightful " (83:26-29) . These characters are divided into two groups: the main character, Morose, whose humour is dilated upon as being a source of variety, liveliness, delight, and the other characters. To remove the possible criticism that the character of Morose is not a just image of nature, Neander says that it is not an imitation of man in general, but of one particular man: ". . . humour is the ridiculous extravagance of conversation, wherein one man differs from all others" (84:17-18) . And again, " by humour is meant some extravagant habit, passion, or affection, particular . . . to some one person, by the oddness of which, he is immediately distinguished from the rest of men " (85:26-29) . In this respect of individuality or particularity the English have excelled not only the *ethos* of the Ancients, which " contained only the general characters of men and manners " (85:13-14) , but also the scanty imitations of the stock characters of Plautus which the French affect in spite of their use of the term *humeur* (85:21-24) . Besides Morose, Neander continues, there are at least nine or ten distinct characters in this play — all of them particular (86:5) and hence representations that are more just than those of the Ancients and the French.

Having spoken so far of the many varied characters as they are all used, with their humours, in the main design, Neander at this point mentions the " writing " of their conversation: " I shall not waste time in commending the writing of this play; but I will give you my opinion, that there is more wit and acuteness of fancy in it than in any [other] of Ben Jonson's " (86:12-15) . He does not tell us how the writing compares with that of the Ancients or of the French. This is not an accidental evasion, for by his second proposition (79:1) he does not need to argue that the writing is good in a regular play; and he has already said that Beaumont and Fletcher best exemplify wit in the age of Shakespeare (81: 24-25) . Later, when Neander speaks of the writing as a very special means of " heightening nature " in serious plays rather than in comedy, he will attempt to show that in wit the playwrights of his own generation—since the Restoration—excel even those of the age of Shakespeare, Beaumont and Fletcher, and Jonson.

Consequently, Neander returns to the "contrivance of this plot" (86:19). It is very elaborate (86:19) and at the same time so artfully managed as to appear inevitable. Furthermore, "this excellent contrivance is still more to be admired, because 'tis comedy, where the persons are . . . not elevated by passions or high concernments as in serious plays" (86:28-32). To write a play that is both just and lively without the easier method of securing liveliness, that of the passions, demands greater art. Still another achievement is the securing of delight through suspense; Jonson has chosen a long-expected day for the action, a device praised by Corneille (87:9-14).[22] Another reason for admiring the contrivance is that Jonson has prepared the spectator for a "humourous" character by giving "a pleasant description of it before the person first appears" (87:26-27). And, finally, Jonson exemplifies a contrivance which Eugenius had noted as absent from the plays of the Ancients: namely, the division of his play by acts rather than by entrances and exits, with "the business of it [rising] in every act" (88:4). Neander concludes that, if this comedy were translated into French prose, the controversy would be decided between the two nations.

Thus the English do have a dramatic poesy. Though it lay buried during the civil wars, since the return of the monarch there have been English plays which "deserve all laurels but the English" (89:5). On the point of judging contemporary plays, Neander recalls (89:22) "an ancient writer," Velleius, as warning him of the difficulties of criticizing that which is too closely admired [23] — the same ancient

[22] Cf. the third discourse, *Œuvres* (1862), I, 116, where Corneille says of the unity of Time: " . . . je ne puis oublier que c'est un grand ornement pour un poëme que le choix d'un jour illustre et attendu depuis quelque temps." Cf. Burrows, *op. cit.*, p. 75.

[23] Velleius Paterculus, II, 36, 3 (Loeb Classical Library, pp. 128-129): " . . . nam vivorum ut magna admiratio, ita censura difficilis est."

writer who was brought in earlier (67:24) as prophesying an *aliquid* wherein "we may conquer." Certainly the *aliquid* has been fulfilled as far as English humours in comedy are concerned. The passions in tragedy will come later, within the requirement of the definition for passions and humours. Here Neander is made to aver simply that, though they yield to a few plays of the last age in England, "so can it be no addition to pronounce of our present poets, that they have far surpassed all the Ancients, and the modern writers of other countries" (89:28-31). Neander's argument for the Moderns and for the English is not complete in time, since "present poets" have not entered the analysis.

Neither is it complete in substance. Although Neander has said something of passions and humours, he has emphasized up to this point the contrivance of Jonson. The other element of the play, writing, which includes the thoughts and the words, must be just, as well as lively.[24] For the English plays the only mentions of writing have been Lisideius' contemptuous dismissal of rime — "our poets write so ill in it" (67:14) — and Neander's assertion that the plays of Shakespeare's period had "more masculine fancy and greater spirit in the writing, than there is in any of the French" (79:3). That is clearly liveliness. Now English writing, particularly in rime, needs to be argued in the same way; Crites will therefore assert that it is not just (true to life), and Neander will argue that rime is not only just (exactly imitating nature in its heightened moods) but also more lively, especially in serious plays;[25] it is "natural" and "more effectual" than blank verse (94:21). Along with the refutations and new points of the various speakers up to this juncture of their friendly argument there is a cumulative effect of what has been granted: Eugenius, the second speaker, accepted Crites' assumption that the Moderns have

[24] George Saintsbury, *History of English Criticism* (Edinburgh, 1925), p. 120, implies that the *Essay* is distorted by this long coda, as he calls it, on rime.

[25] Dryden (not Neander) admits that this part of the *Essay* is weak. In the *Defence* he wrote that his brother-in-law "attacks me on my weakest side, my defence of verse" (112: 16-17). Thus it was not entirely inconsistent on Dryden's part to give up rime ten years later in a play that proposed to imitate the style of Shakespeare, *All for Love*.

profited by the rules of the Ancients (43:22-24); Lisideius, before taking up the French drama, granted Crites the same thing (56:33); and Neander, before refuting Lisideius, acknowledged the virtues of the French and the faults of the English in contrivance (67:28-33). These concepts have been constantly brought forward. The essential division of the elements of a play into contrivance and writing, and the gradual movement from ancient to modern, from instruction to delight, from just to lively, from nature to art — what else can complete the argument except a third and final section on English contemporary heroic verse? [26]

III

Crites, after closing the argument between Lisideius and Neander by granting that "the most material things that can be said have been already urged on either side" (90: 2-3), disagrees with both opponents for assuming "that rhyme is proper for the stage" (90:7). In limiting his argument against rime he grants that it has had a long and not ignoble history in England. He also is not interested in whether England got it from France or France from England. He will limit the discussion concerning rime to serious plays (90:21), since Neander not only has tacitly agreed with him that rime is not good in comedy (78) but also has omitted writing from the defence of Ben Jonson's comedy.

Crites' arguments, which Dryden adapts to the scheme of the *Essay* from Howard's preface to *Four New Plays* (1665), are mainly two: that rime is unnatural. the inference being that it is not an ornament to the quickness of repartee in argumentative verse; and that rime does not circumscribe too luxuriant a fancy (91:35 ff. and 93:8 ff.) .[27] Again Crites, in character, leans more toward the justness of the definition than toward the liveliness. Under the first

[26] Though Dryden's preface to *The Rival Ladies* (1664) is part of the background for the section on rime, its arguments are so much more clearly brought out in the *Defence of the Essay* that a separate analysis of the earlier preface has not been thought necessary here.

[27] D. D. Arundell, ed., *Dryden and Howard: 1664-1668* (Cambridge, 1929), p. 9.

point he argues that, if art imitates nature, then the language that is closest to nature, namely, that nearest ordinary conversation, is best; while elevation is proper, the "most constrained" way of speaking (i.e. in rime) is not. And he quotes Aristotle to lend his argument authority (91:21).[28] Though Aristotle had said that iambic verse is nearest conversation, Crites assumes this to be the equivalent in English of blank verse, and concludes from this that blank verse numbers "are fittest for a play; the others for a paper of verses, or a poem" (91:26). That Dryden is here joining in an argument with his brother-in-law is suggested by this contemptuous phrase he puts into Crites' mouth about the "paper of verses," for in the preceding year in his dedication of *Annus Mirabilis* to his brother-in-law Dryden had written of his poem to the Duchess: "Some, who have seen a paper of verses, which I wrote last year to her Highness the Duchess, have accused them of that only thing I could defend in them" (18:30-33). In this section of the *Essay* Crites most nearly approximates Howard. Crites' first argument is boiled down to this: blank verse, being "nearer to nature," is preferable to rime. His reasoning is that a play should be a just imitation of nature; liveliness is omitted.

The inference from his first argument,[29] concerning repartee, continues this argument that rime does not lend itself to a just image of the language of real men. Rime, Crites avers, spoils the effect of deception because it makes repartee look like a confederacy between two characters, unlike repartee in real life (92:15). For Crites the probability rests largely in the imitation of the language of real men: "For a play is still an imitation of Nature; we know we are to be deceived, and we desire to be so; but no man ever was deceived but with a probability of truth; for who will suffer a gross lie to be fastened on him" (92:23-27)? At this point by bringing in an analogy of the scenery, he exposes

---

[28] Actually Aristotle says (*Poetics*, 1449a 18) that the iambic is the most conversational of all meters but that when we rise above the ordinary pitch of conversation we speak in hexameters—which, after all, is Neander's, not Crites', point. Cf. Neander's argument, 97:19 ff.

[29] In his refutation Neander calls this "the inference of your first argument" (100:15).

himself to the charge that he is condemning not the thing
but the manner of the thing. This analogy is taken directly
from Howard's preface to *Four New Plays:* "But such may
as well excuse an ill scene that is not naturally painted because they know 'tis only a scene and not really a city or
country."[30] Another kind of impropriety, besides making
"high thoughts" unnatural, is that rime is too majestic for
"low thoughts"; and Crites alludes to the tag about "shut-
ting the door" (93:8), which later Dryden uses to pulverize
Howard by dwelling upon his mistake in Latin (116:30–
117:24).

Crites' second argument (93:8) is also an old point of
difference between the two relatives; it was first mentioned
by Dryden in his preface to *The Rival Ladies* (8:2-26).
Now it is made a negative argument: rime does not circumscribe the liveliness of the poet's imagination. Thus Dryden
here makes Crites argue against him, to the effect that a man
who lacks judgment will lack it as much in rime as out of it:
Ovid wrote in Latin verse but wrote loosely, whereas Jonson
wrote out of rime yet tightly.

Neander refutes these two arguments against rime in the
same order in which Crites gave them: rime can be made
natural in itself, and thus it may be inferred that it can be
natural or proper in a play of repartee (95:8 and 100:15);
and rime does act as a control to the fancy (105:19).

With deference "to that person from whom you have
borrowed your strongest arguments" (94:11), meaning, of
course, Sir Robert (cf. 94:1 and 106:17), Neander first of
all limits his side of the discussion. He will exclude all comedy
from his defence of rime, because comedy has already been
dealt with and because it does not need the "just heightening" which is rime's greatest reason for being. Furthermore,
Neander does not deny that blank verse may also be used
(94:16). He intends to show "that in serious plays where
the subject and the characters are great, and the plot
unmixed with mirth . . . rhyme is there as natural and more
effectual than blank verse" (94:17-21), where the term

[30] Arundell, *op. cit.*, p. 9.

"natural" enters by reason of the justness and the term "more effectual" by reason of the liveliness of the definition.

Then he takes up Crites' first argument against rime— that it is not natural—by accusing Crites of condemning not the thing but the manner. There are defects in ill rime as there are in ill blank verse. A good poet must exercise care and art (95:26), for whether he is writing in blank verse or in heroic couplets, he is never forced to say what he would not otherwise say (95:25). And what he says in verse — if care is exercised — does not shock the listener into think- ing that it is contrary to common speaking (95:1). If, then, rime is natural in itself, it will be natural in a play depend- ing upon the "well placing of the words." As for Crites' quotation of Aristotle (91:22), Neander can easily refute that as an argument (96:24) by saying that we are talking not of classical meters but of English verse; numbers or quantity constituted the classical meters but in English verse there are other means of measuring, and rime is the chief distinction (97:4). Furthermore, rime can be made as near prose as blank verse by enjambement (97:22) or by em- ploying other devices to vary the "chime of the couplet," as in D'Avenant's *Siege of Rhodes* (97:26). A final reason why rime is appropriate to a serious play is that it is one way left open by which we can hope to outdo Jonson, Fletcher, and Shakespeare — the *aliquid* which Lisideius noted in his quotation from Velleius (67:24), which Neander has already fulfilled by the contrivance of humours *for the last age*, and which he here fulfills by rime in the writing *of this age:* "This therefore will be a good argument to us, either not to write at all, or to attempt some other way. There is no bays to be expected in their walks" (99:16-19). Rime, in other words, is produced by the "genius of the age"; it is one means in our age of imitating the new nature (99:26).

This brings Neander to Crites' inference from the first argument, that rime is not natural (100:15). Crites had inferred that rime was improbable in dialogue, particularly where there was repartee. Neander refutes this by saying that it depends on whether one is writing a comedy or a

serious play. Comedy being near to nature, prose is best.
A serious play, on the other hand, is "indeed the representation of Nature, but 'tis Nature wrought up to an higher
pitch" (100:31-32). Consequently, heroic verse, being a
more heightened form of language, is more natural for serious
plays than is blank verse or prose. The argument is not
against blank verse *per se*, as Neander pointed out at the
beginning; it is against blank verse as the most just means,
the means of attaining the most exact imitation, for example,
of the speech of noble persons whose passions are aroused.
In this respect, Neander says, Crites' arguments against
heroic couplets in repartee or dialogue are as strong in epic
as in tragedy (101:16 ff.). And here is one reason why the
definition of a play was purposely *a genere et fine* (36:10).
Neander at this point alludes to Lisideius' definition, and
points out that epic and tragedy (comedy having already
been made to fit) also fit the definition: "The *genus* of them
is the same, a just and lively image of human nature, in its
actions, passions, and traverses of fortune; so is the end,
namely, for the delight and benefit of mankind" (101:26-29).
The main difference, and for the first time the *differentia*
of "acted rather than narrated" becomes explicit, is that
tragedy is by its very nature a more lively image than epic:
"Tragedy performs it *viva voce*, or by action, in dialogue;
wherein it excels the Epic Poem, which does it chiefly by
narration, and therefore is not so lively an image of human
nature" (101:32-102:2). As a consequence, a play to be
an "image of nature" must be not only just but also lively;
if it is an image of "high nature," it must be set above
ordinary nature. Rime secures that effect of heightening.

But what of Crites' inference concerning repartee? Although it is already answered, Neander closes in upon his
opponent (102:17). The same objection Crites makes to
repartee in rime might be made to repartee in blank verse;
moreover, the finishing of a line of repartee in verse by
another speaker was never held to be a mistake in the classical authors. Rime at present is the substitute for quantity
in classical meters (103:5). As for repartee, truly it is art
(103:24), and as art it is just in so far as it is "an high

imitation of Nature in those sudden gusts of passion" (103: 26-27); but repartee is also lively because it has a "quick and poynant brevity" in it. Rime adds to repartee "the last perfection" (104:3). Since it still involves a choice of words, to avoid vulgarity the poet can make even the lowest thought appear lofty. Even if "unlock the door" be vulgar in household conversation, Seneca in imitating that bit of speech had occasion to make it sound "high and lofty in his Latin" (105:4). If we can do this in rime, Neander implies, rime besides being just, is also a means to liveliness of spirit.

Finally (105:19), Neander refutes Crites' other argument against rime—that it does not curb a luxuriant fancy. Crites had maintained (from Howard's preface to *Four New Plays*) that a poet of judgment did not need to curb his fancy. Neander objects to the use of the term "judgment"; he who has an infallible judgment will commit faults neither in rime nor out of it, and he who has a crazed judgment will be beyond the help of rime or any other means. No writer can fail to profit by subordinate aids to his judgment (107:4); and verse, Neander affirms, is one of these aids. Thus rime helps to make the image just.

The problem in *An Essay of Dramatic Poesy* was the complete exploration of the contrivance and writing of a play by examples in ancient and modern drama in order to determine which nation has the best. The problem has been solved. By this time the barge stood still at the foot of Somerset stairs, and, the pleasant conversation over, the four friends parted company. What they said and the way they said it has since secured fame for Dryden as a critic and master of prose, but his brother-in-law, Sir Positive, took immediate issue.

CHAPTER III

THE DEFENCE AGAINST HOWARD

"... they cannot be good poets, who are
not accustomed to argue well" (121: 21-22).

THERE is no reason to suspect that Dryden's simple
account (133: 7 ff.) of the quarrel with Sir Robert
Howard is not the true one. Dryden had defended the
couplet in the preface to *The Rival Ladies* (1664); Howard
answered this in his preface to *Four New Plays* (1665);
Dryden replied, impersonally, in the *Essay;* Howard rejoined
in his preface to *The Duke of Lerma* (1668); and Dryden
closes the quarrel in a devastating *Defence of An Essay
of Dramatic Poesy*, which he prefixed to the second edition
of *The Indian Emperor* (1668). Only when forced to, does
Dryden become personal in his attack.[1] After dealing this
crushing blow, he gave up the quarrel, and omitted this
diatribe from further editions of *The Indian Emperor*.

Since the immediate purpose of the *Defence* is to answer
Howard's preface to *The Duke of Lerma*, as indicated by
the subtitle, it will be well to examine that preface briefly.
In it Howard, after stating how he came to write the play
he is introducing, asserts that he will retire from the theater
because he feels incapable of writing the kind of play —
in plot and verse — now demanded. This demand, he implies strongly, is not that of the audience, but rather of some
critics (meaning, of course, Dryden): "I rather blame the

---

[1] For further facts in the relationship between Dryden and Sir Robert Howard
see W. S. Clark, " Dryden's Relations with Howard and Orrery." *Modern Language Notes*, 42 (1927), 16-20.

unnecessary understanding of some that have laboured to give strict rules to things that are not mathematical." [2] It is taste alone, in Howard's opinion, not strict rules, which should prescribe in such matters: "For in the difference of tragedy and comedy, and of farce itself, there can be no determination but by the taste, nor in the manner of their composure." [3] From this point he attempts to refute what Dryden says, first, about rime, then about the unities. He himself wrote some scenes of *The Duke of Lerma* in rime, some in blank verse—as his taste dictated. But Dryden had tried, in his *Essay*, to "prove rhyme as natural in a serious play, and more effectual, than blank verse." [4] The word "natural," Howard continues, is wrongly applied: "For 'tis not the question, whether rhyme or not rhyme is best or most natural for a grave and serious subject, but what is nearest the nature of that which it presents." [5] The difference between the two men as far as the suitability of rime is concerned is, then, the difference between two definitions of the usually ill-defined norm "nature." Because Dryden's *Defence* clarifies the main points of his *Essay* and consequently of his theory of drama, it will pay us to review these differences. Through such "occasional" controversy, Dryden demands that greater attention be paid to the foundation of his critical platform.

Dryden had himself made fun (6: 32) of the pomposity of some rimes for ordinary occasions, and had granted that such rimes were "un-natural," i.e. they were bad because the word choice was bad, or because the poet placed the word at the end merely for the sake of its rime. Howard had used (in his earlier preface to *Four New Plays*) as an example of silly riming the theoretical situation of a master bidding in pompous couplets his servant to "close the door." [6] Dryden, in return, had found for that part of his *Essay* dealing with this subject a quotation from Seneca (105: 6) almost fitting Howard's theoretical example, except that the Latin was *reserate* ("to open") rather than "to close."

---

[2] D. D. Arundel, ed., *Dryden and Howard: 1664-1668* (Cambridge, 1929), p. 94.

[3] *Ibid.*   [4] *Ibid.*, p. 95.   [5] *Ibid.*   [6] *Ibid.*, p. 9.

And here Howard grants that Seneca's sonorous Latin does make something out of so bald a command as "shut the door." The mistake of "closing" for "opening" was pardonable, since Howard's initial example was "closing," but Dryden will not miss the chance to exploit this trivial error. In the first part of his preface, then, Howard argues that rime is natural or unnatural as it imitates impassioned or ordinary conversation, and that it does not depend upon whether the poet is writing comedy or tragedy. Hence his emphasis upon taste rather than upon genre.

From the problem of rime Howard goes to his second main point: "But if we examine the general rules laid down for plays by strict reason, we shall find the errors equally gross."[7] Again he bases his argument on the premise that Dryden has misunderstood the term "natural." To Howard the term "nature" has the same signification whether it is applied to empirical reality or to a representation of that reality. On this basis he attempts to overthrow Dryden's "great foundation" by examining his rules for the unity of Place and Time (which we have discovered are not Dryden's "great foundation" but only a partial means to a partial end of a play). Cramping a play into a single place or into twenty-four hours of time, writes Howard, is called natural: "For that is concluded most natural which is most probable to that which it presents."[8] But people who argue for the unities of Place and Time, Howard asserts, are arguing for degrees of impossibility. A single place or a limited time is not "natural": "For, all being impossible, they are none of them nearest the truth or nature of what they present. For impossibilities are all equal, and admit no degrees."[9] Concluding with a rather clumsy play of gallantry, Howard accepts Dryden's stricture concerning rime—that those against it are usually inept in it, and, with transparent unbelief, he confesses at the end: "none has written in that way better than himself [Dryden] nor few worse than I."

Dryden's main problem is to defend his *Essay* against these animadversions. Consequently, like the preface of

[7] *Ibid.*, p. 96.   [8] *Ibid.*, p. 96.   [9] *Ibid.*, p. 97.

Howard, his problem is double: to defend his original statement that rime is natural in serious plays and to show that
the dramatic rules as set down by Aristotle, Horace, Corneille, and Jonson are not erroneous when properly understood. The division demanded by this double problem occurs
at the paragraph beginning: "And now I come to the boldest
part of his discourse" (122: 12). But before taking up
Dryden's arguments, it would be well to consider for a
moment how these two problems, thus linked fortuitously
by Howard, actually are part of Dryden's whole design in
the *Essay*. Though distinct in Howard and, for the purposes
of argument, in Dryden, they are nevertheless closely con-
nected. Dryden's answer follows exactly Howard's order of
argument. He purposely avails himself of his brother-in-
law's methods. For example, Dryden asserts that Howard
"discovers not his whole design at once" (112: 15), but
intending to attack a fundamental premise, he seems to aim
only at Dryden and at Dryden's weakest side, the defence
of rime (112: 16). So Dryden appears at first to be attack-
ing only Howard's rather inept arguments against rime,
whereas in actuality he is clarifying his central theory of
drama, that it is an "image of human nature" (it is human
nature in action that the poet must imitate well), for the
end of instructing through delight (113: 29-33). The arrangement of the argument, furthermore, has the advantage of
passing from that which is most easily accepted to that
which is more abstruse, from the outward manifestation of
drama—the dialogue—to its very foundation. Dryden bal-
ances one part against the other part, also, in moving from
that which concerns him personally to that which concerns
ancient, modern, and possibly future dramatists. By this
order he advances from what he terms his weakest side to
what by implication is his strongest, from an accident of
drama, dependent upon the occasion and the particular audience, to that which is essential to all drama, from that which
he can easily give up, to that which no poet writing a play
can possibly give up since it is demanded by the nature of
the art he is creating. Finally, the two problems form a
fundamental division in Dryden's treatment of the "parts

of a play": one has to do with "writing," the other with "contrivance." The order which he used to advantage in the *Essay* is here temporarily changed because of the immediate necessity of answering Howard's preface to *The Duke of Lerma,* and for reasons of emphasis.

The basis of his argument is one and the same for both assertions: a play is not "nature," that is, actual reality; it is a representation or image or imitation of that actual reality. This basis he asserts twice in the *Defence* with special application to each of the two problems. For the first, that of rime, his basis of argument is this:

> As for what he urges, that *a play will still be supposed to be a composition of several persons speaking* ex tempore, *and that good verses are the hardest things which can be imagined to be so spoken;* I must crave leave to dissent from his opinion, as to the former part of it: for, if I am not deceived, a play is supposed to be the work of the poet, imitating or representing the conversation of several persons; and this I think to be as clear, as he thinks the contrary (114: 3-11).

The premise stated for the second problem, that concerning "rules," not only is identical but emphasizes the unity of the *Essay of Dramatic Poesy* which this *Defence* explains:

> I never heard of any other foundation of Dramatic Poesy than the imitation of Nature; neither was there ever pretended any other by the Ancients or Moderns, or me, who endeavour to follow them in that rule. This I have plainly said in my definition of a play; that it is a just and lively image of human nature, &c (123: 4-10).

Though Dryden appeals to authority for the truth of this assumption, he does not cite authority for authority's sake; he appeals to our ordinary experience and practice, to common sense, and to his own taste and literary appreciation gained from his studies of literatures ancient and modern. That the statements cited above are the basis of his argument is easy to see. The "imitation of nature" is all-inclusive, taking into its confines both parts of his argument; it is that which is most likely to be conceded; remove it and the entire structure of the *Defence* falls; and, finally, it best serves the avowed purpose of the argument, to defend the *Essay of Dramatic Poesy,* by citing the very core of that essay—the definition of a play.

The first problem is this: Dryden had said that rime is best or most "natural" in a serious play. Howard attempted to refute this. But Dryden finds Howard misstating the question (112: 23-31). By misstating it Howard makes this invalid inference from a true premise: verse is more remote from actual conversation than prose (true), therefore, no serious play ought to be written in verse (false). Then, after thus showing that Howard has failed to break down his original assertion, Dryden gives more reasons why his original assertion is true. This is the crux of his proof, and all the persiflage and air of superiority and personal attacks upon Howard do not obscure it. Dryden sniffs the air of battle like a champion knight (111: 15); he declares he is willing to bow to an adversary so bold as to take up the weaker side (111: 11). He hits at his opponent's reputation as Sir Positive (111: 23), and thus strengthens his own position of being sceptical and unwilling to go any further than the audience demands in rime (116: 4) or practice decrees in contrivance (123: 28).

Dryden reiterates his original statement that rime is best in serious plays. This being a play, there is a poet and an audience. To prove that verse is "natural" in plays (the meaning temporarily unqualified — 113: 21) is impossible; it is merely sufficient to show that verse helps to fulfill the major end of drama, delight; and that it does this by heightening the limitation of actuality: "'Tis true, that to imitate well is a poet's work; but to affect the soul, and excite the passions, and, above all, to move admiration (which is the delight of serious plays), a bare imitation will not serve" (113: 29-33). Dryden will go further and, with the aid of an analogy from painting, assert on the basis of his premise that one reason why prose is not to be used in serious plays is that it is too near the "nature" which it represents (114: 15). He quotes Horace's "Ut pictura poesis" to support this, and uses as an example Jonson's plays. If that writer's *Bartholomew Fair* were exactly like an actual fair, in its conversation, then the fair would give the same pleasure "to an ingenious person" as the play does (115: 2-4). The history of drama, again, shows how in the actual practice of writing plays, prose has been deposed (115: 14 ff.). The Ancients used verse, which by modern writers has been displaced by rime—as a means to the end of pleasing (116: 3).

Quibble though Dryden's diatribe on Howard's " bad Latin " is, its function is to undermine Howard's argument by showing how easily Howard would misstate the fundamental question. The same function is fulfilled by Dryden's hitting upon the large number of errata in Howard's play as printed (177: 25 ff.). Continuing *ad nauseam* with this personal abuse, Dryden makes fun of Howard's " farewell to the Muses " (118: 32) — " the corruption of a poet is the generation of a statesman " (119: 13-14).[10]

In all of this he is making ready now to pass from his problem of rime to his problem of the unities, and he harps finally upon Howard's mistakes of judgment: " We shall see him now as great a critic as he was a poet, and the reason why he excelled so much in poetry will be evident, for it will appear to have proceeded from the exactness of his judgment " (119: 32-35). A convenient bridge between the two problems is Howard's assertion that the difference between the kinds of plays lies not in their composition but in taste. This argument Howard used at the beginning of his preface. Dryden's removing it from the position it had can be explained by his need to prepare for what is to come. For his whole argument depends upon the issue, first, that they are arguing about a play, and, secondly, that they are arguing about a serious play. Howard's assertion that taste makes the only difference is " so manifest an error, that I need not lose time to contradict it " (120: 8-9). Whether a poet is writing a comedy or a tragedy, the end should be taken into account—to please the audience (120: 33-34); but a play is good or bad beyond the taste of a particular audience. It does not follow that the audience invariably is pleased by good

[10] " R. F." (perhaps Richard Flecknoe), who answered Dryden's *Defence* in Sir Robert's silence (cf. Macdonald's No. 159), attempts to turn this epigram about. Dryden was the son of a committeeman and in the political employ of Sir Gilbert Pickering: thus " . . . it may be more properly applied to the Squire [Dryden], that the corruption of a statesman is the generation of a poet-laureate." Cf. Malone's additions in James M. Osborn, *John Dryden: Some Biographical Facts and Problems* (New York, 1940), p. 123.

plays, or that the plays which do please are necessarily good plays (120:34–121:1). Tastes differ with the age.

Before Dryden comes to the second half of his problem— that of the "rules of contrivance" which Howard objected to —he says something of the nature of proof and of argument. Howard had written that it was not necessary that poets should study strict reason (121:14-15). Dryden replies that "false reasonings and colours of speech [hitting at Howard's false inferences and obscure language] are the certain marks of one who does not understand the stage": "... they cannot be good poets, who are not accustomed to argue well" (121:20-24). A play must resemble "natural truth," of course, but the poet "dresses truth" and "adorns nature" (121:27). To do this he must have intellectual fiber as well as variety of fancy and sweetness of expression. Ovid had the latter only, but Virgil possessed both the judgment and the fancy (122:1-4).

This brings Dryden to his second and main problem: "And now I come to the boldest part of his discourse, wherein he attacks not me, but all the Ancients and Moderns; and undermines, as he thinks, the very foundations on which Dramatic Poesy is built" (122:12-15). Dryden quotes Howard once more to show that he has mistaken what Dryden denominated as the means for the foundation (122: 30-34). To Dryden the "rules" are means (123:30-33). The foundation, as we have seen in previously quoting the basis of his argument (123:4-10), is that a play is an "imitation of human nature"—the generic means to the end of delight: "having laid down, that Nature is to be imitated, and that proposition proving the next, that then there are means which conduce to the imitating of Nature, I dare proceed no further positively" (123:26-29). In the *Essay* "I have only laid down some opinions of the Ancients and Moderns, and of my own, as means which they used, and which I thought probable for the attaining of that end" (123:29-32). Related to this confusion of means and end is the meaning of the term "natural." Howard interpreted the term to mean "nearest to Nature," that is, most resembling the actual world. Dryden, on the other hand, used

the term in a sense pertaining to the "nature" of a play—
rime, for example, was shown to be "natural" in that it was
appropriate to the ends for which a play exists. Dryden
never said that people in actual life speak heroic couplets.
Howard seemed to overlook Dryden's insistence that a play
is a "just and lively image of human nature."

This mistaking of means for end Dryden shows by quoting what Howard wrote concerning the unities of Time and
Place (124: 3-13). Before Dryden refutes Howard's statement, he takes exception to Howard's implication that he
(Dryden) is magisterial. He insists upon the meaning of
the word "essay," and that his work was anything but
magisterial, for the whole discourse was sceptical (124: 18–
125: 15). Dryden requotes his dedication to Lord Buckhurst,
being careful to omit his misquotation of Tacitus (125: 2;
27: 7); and once more he quotes his advertisement to the
reader of the *Essay*. That his opponent has the kind of
reputation he desires to be free of is shown by what may be
an allusion to Shadwell's nickname for Howard—Sir Positive
(125: 18).

Again quoting from Howard's preface the portions concerning the arguments against the unities of Place and Time,
he abbreviates, first, the argument against Place (126: 9 ff.),
manifestly not a syllogism: if one stage cannot be two places,
then there is no such thing as the unity of Place, and consequently Dryden is wrong. But, writes Dryden, "I plainly
deny his minor proposition" (126: 21), because it depends
upon a false assumption. Of course, one stage cannot be two
places, but that one stage can "represent" two places successively is plain when a distinction is made between the
"real" and the "imaginary" place (126: 30). Once more
Dryden appeals to the common consent for the truth of his
assertion that the stage can represent imaginary places successively (127: 11-12). All that Dryden implied in citing
certain opinions concerning this means to the end of "imitation" is that the closer the two imaginary places are
together, the more likely the reason is to accept them. Thus
to be accused of saying that one place can actually be two
is as absurd as to be accused of saying that men speak rime.

Hence, if Howard will grant that there is a difference between the real place (or theater) and the imaginary place of the action (let us say Athens), then he will have to grant the corollary that it is possible to "represent" more than one place on the stage successively (127: 23). The imagination and the reason of the poet must both be brought into play — the imagination daring to "represent" successive places, but the reason pulling the imagination back from wandering too far: "Fancy and Reason go hand in hand; the first cannot leave the last behind, and though Fancy, when it sees the wide gulf, would venture over, as the nimbler, yet it is withheld by Reason, which will refuse to take the leap, when the distance over it appears too large" (128: 18–23). In this way, though the real place is the theater and the imaginary place is Athens, the imagination may be given the latitude to wander, possibly, anywhere within the city limits, but not to jump between acts from Athens to Syracuse!

The same kinds of argument are employed against Howard's refusal to grant that the unity of Time is valid. Here, as in Place, the proportion is between the actual or "real" time of the performance and the imaginary time of the action. It is absurd to think that Dryden or anyone who has talked on the unities would suppose twenty-four hours of action is the same as three hours of performance. But the reason will the sooner accept the imaginary action of twenty-four hours, as represented by three hours' actual time, than it would accept twenty-four years as represented by three hours' actual time. The fallacy of Howard's arguments against both unities, Dryden summarizes, is shown by the analogy of the looking-glass: it does not have to be as large as the things it can represent.

Thus Dryden is far less magisterial than Crites. In spite of his own animadversions against Howard's freedom with the "time" of *The Duke of Lerma*, Dryden argues for the dramatic unities not as rules to be blindly followed on authority, but as specific means to the generic means (imitation) to the end of delight. The unities of Place and Time are derived by Dryden not from the characteristics either of the real object of imitation or of imitation itself, but from the psychological nature of men as spectators of plays. They are treated in relation not to imitation (as the unity of Action is in Aristotle), but to the end or effect of plays (the rhetorical approach of Horace and Quintilian). Most of Dryden's critical dicta upon the unities are brought to a close here. Little is to be gained by quoting stray passages and concluding that Dryden "upheld" the unities, or was "influenced" by Aristotle or Corneille in so doing. He looks upon them as means of contrivance (which is not the whole play), means that secure more justness than liveliness, demanding more judgment from poet and audience than imagination. The unities are only part of a whole.

Dryden, in this essay, sticks close to Howard's preface. His last point, on rime once more (132: 29), was Howard's last point too. Thus Dryden has proved his double contention: that rime is more "natural" than prose in serious plays because by heightening that which it represents it better attains the end of delight; and that the "contrivances" of Place and Time are not, as Howard said they were, merely "degrees of impossibility." The rime is a means to a lively image of human nature, and the rules help to make it a just one. Howard did not argue well, and he was not a very good poet.

CHAPTER IV

THE SIGNIFICANCE

" . . . mine be like the whetstone's aid,
Which, blunt itself, lends sharpness to the blade."

THIS couplet, which Dryden and Soames were to translate from Horace's *Ars Poetica* (304-305), appears in Latin on the title page of the first edition of Dryden's *Essay of Dramatic Poesy*. Now that we have seen how the *Essay* came to be, what its argument is, and how Dryden defended it, we may well ask, "Where does it take us?" By his choice of problem and by his handling of it, Dryden shows us that he is not discussing the dramatic art in and by and for itself. Drama is not judged according to universal human values, or as an isolated subject matter *in vacuo*. In spite of the fact that he alludes to Aristotle, it is Horace and Quintilian who are his true masters; and drama as rhetoric, in the sense of persuading, influencing, or moving a particular audience by means of language, is his main concern, rather than ethics, poetics, or the literary mind. Thus with greater justification than usual may we concern ourselves with implications.

In the first place, the crisp sentences of Dryden here alone might secure his place in literature. Before 1660 English prose was still, even in the hands of such masters as the translators of King James, definitely dated. Either it was sententious to the point of being jejune, like that of Bacon, or a bit fulsome, like the prose of Browne or Milton. Only after the restoration of Charles II did English prose become the precise and beautifully modulated instrument that it is at its best today. And Dryden's *Essay*, modeled, so Dryden

said, on the periods of Tillotson,[1] is one of the first monu-
ments of English prose which, though written in the seventeenth century, does not seem quaint.

But a piece of literature can transcend even its own dress.
Behind this *Essay* lie a mind and an imagination disciplined
by the study of grammar, rhetoric, and logic, softened by
family affection, fortified by a reading in three literatures,
and sharpened by literary, political, and religious controversy. Doctor Johnson said it was a mind "always curious,
always active, to which every understanding was proud to be
associated, and of which everyone solicited the regard by an
ambitious display of himself."[2]   And the same critic, who
made a description of a man's mind part of his biography,
had also this to say: "Dryden appears to have had a mind
very comprehensive by nature, and much enriched with acquired knowledge.   His compositions are the effects of a
vigorous genius operating upon large materials."[3]   To have
read the *Essay* carefully is to have shared a conversation
with such a man, who without effort ranges from the poetry
of his proem, which has been compared favorably with any
proem of Plato's, to the most vigorous application of the
powers of reason to the discovery of an abstract truth.
The more carefully he is read, the less evidence is there for
accusing him of plagiarism and inconsistency.

Thus the *Essay* has implications for Dryden's whole
theory of drama.   An analysis of his argument reveals how
important to it is a basis of argument, without which there
can be no possibility of demonstration.   In some such way
the *Essay* itself forms a basis for almost all his arguments
on dramatic subjects from 1668 until the last year of his life,
when in 1700 he wrote the preface to the *Fables*.   As the
unity of the *Essay* is the definition of a play — "A just and
lively image of human nature, representing its passions and
humours, and the changes of fortune to which it is subject.

---

[1] William Congreve, *The Dramatick Works of John Dryden* (London, 1717),
II, 19.
[2] Samuel Johnson, "Dryden," in *Lives of the English Poets*, ed. G. B. Hill
(Oxford, 1905), I, 331-481, paragraph 241.
[3] *Ibid.*, paragraphs 321-322.

for the delight and instruction of mankind "— so the *Essay* as a whole gives unity to Dryden's dramatic criticism.

His later essays on dramatic subjects amplify the definition which he thus worked out at the very beginning of his career. Having first defined "a play" in the *Essay* in general terms, he later develops specific definitions for kinds of plays — comedy, heroic drama, and tragedy. Starting with "human nature" as something to be represented in dramatic form, the poet invents plot (changes of fortune) and characters (passions and humours) which he disposes (note the Quintilian terms) in his play; then he expresses these in a style, or elocution. The parts of a play, whatever the genre, are usually divided between "contrivance" and "writing." "Fancy" and "judgment" in varying measures are demanded of the poet. And these two faculties are exercised not only in the formulation of his plot and characters, but in the writing of his wit and rime. The audience can expect to be "instructed" through being "delighted" in the differing senses of those terms for comedy, heroic play, and tragedy which Dryden gives us. The emphasis upon genre arises from the rhetorical view of poesy, the genre providing the occasion or purpose of the author in producing an effect upon a particular audience.

This unity can be illustrated by the harmony between his first great utterance here in 1668 and the last important dramatic preface, that to *Troilus and Cressida* in 1679. Between these two points Dryden does not develop in the sense of undergoing a change in doctrine. He develops only in the sense of filling in previously arrived-at positions and of clarifying certain views. He will insist on liveliness, for example; and when other traits of the play provide that liveliness better than rime can, then he will give up rime. Rime is, like the unities, only a means to an end; and that Dryden's theory of verse still stands may be vouched for by such present-day dramatists as Archibald MacLeish and T. S. Eliot, who have used dramatic poesy for the same effect. Between these two essays Dryden passes from one emphasis to another within the general framework of his theory. Thus the "foundation" and the "superstructure," which in the preface to *Troilus and Cressida* form the basis of his argument that Fletcher's and Shakespeare's tragedies contain something worthy of imitation, are in part determined by the "just and lively" of the *Essay of Dramatic Poesy*.

Essentially, then, Dryden's theory of drama lies in the two major terms which help resolve his fundamental problem of what is a good play—a good play is a "just and lively" representation, and this unity of doctrine seems to reconcile what in the past have been taken to be contradictions in his work. Practically every statement in Dryden's critical prefaces is justified therein by its relationship to one or to the other of these contrary terms, or to their combination. As for Dryden's attitude toward his predecessors, for example, he would grant Shakespeare all the "liveliness" he himself would have liked to attain, but with Voltaire he deplored the great poet's looseness of structure and lack of decorum. There is no paradox in this, nor in his admiration for Jonson and his love for Shakespeare. In the entire theory both the rules of the dramatic unities and the Longinian scope of his plea for bold metaphors and for the play of passions have a fitting place. The rules (and we have thought we could get along without rules) make for a just imitation; the metaphors (and we distrust poetry) make mostly for a lively one. Dryden's *Essay of Dramatic Poesy* can still be a whetstone that sharpens our steel.

DATE DUE

APR 2 '87			